Beyond the Dark Cloud

Beyond the Dark Cloud

Copyright ©2023 Maritza Mejias-Ditzenberger
ISBN 13: 979-8-218-26847-3
Library of Congress Control Number: 2023915119

Edited by Michele Chynoweth and Carlene Roche
Typeset by Helen Ounjian
Cover design by 99Designs
Drawing of Young Maritza by Sara J. Wozniak

This work depicts actual events of the author, recalled and recorded as truthfully as permitted to remain consistent with the recollection. Dialogue may be embellished but within the nature of the character depicted. Names of characters have been changed to respect their privacy.

Printed in the United States of America

Perfect Misfits LLC
An Independent Publishing Company
For inquiries, email perfectmisfits.de@gmail.com

Perfect Misfits LLC
An Independent Publishing Company

Maritza Mejias-Ditzenberger

BEYOND THE DARK CLOUD

Conquering Anxiety & Depression: A Memoir

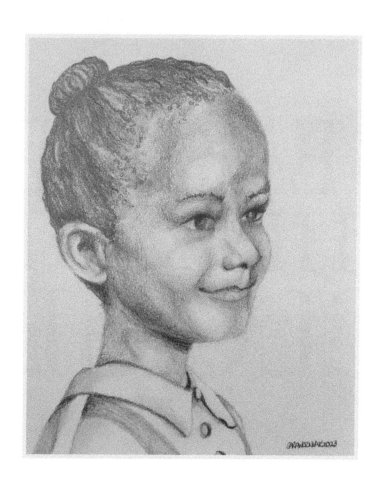

"I sought the LORD, and He heard me, and delivered me from all of my fears."

Psalms 34:4 (KJV)

This book is dedicated to Mami, who was always present for me in my toughest moments and helped me get through them with a laugh. I love you Lucy!

This book is also dedicated to those who suffer from anxiety and depression and those who have conquered it. We are a family of dreamers, sensitive hearts, world changers and stronghold breakers!

My Thanks

I would like to thank my wonderful husband, Lance Ditzenberger, who supported this work from the beginning. I am so grateful to God for you. You are a little girl's answered prayer many times over. I love you forever.

To my brothers and sisters, you guys have always made me feel protected, loved and that I was not crazy. Your generous hearts of love will be a reminder and comfort to me all the days of my life. Thank you. I look forward to many more laughs with you guys!

For Papi

Papi, thank you for showing me unconditional love. Thank you for showing me what forgiveness really looks like and for your constant love. You never have to be afraid any longer for God holds you in the palm of His Hand, and He won't let go. Te quiero mucho. -maricita

And finally, but definitely not in the least, I dedicate this book to the little girl in me who lived with so many fears. You've come a long way, mama and I'm proud of you. As you walk away from me now, one hand holding on to His, you look back at me and smile. You are in the light now. I release you to be forever healed and happy. Although I know, you will always be a part of me, you are free now to walk Beyond the Dark Cloud. Thank you for believing in me. We are both free. I love you.

Table of Contents

Preface

Let me just start with this—depression and anxiety can suck the life out of you. I think anyone who has ever experienced their effects would agree. Everyday tasks can be a struggle, but day in and day out we who suffer from anxiety and depression somehow make it through. With depression, days pass by like shadows. There is no sunlight, no reprieve. It's like someone hit the stop button on the elevator of your life. Trying to accomplish routine daily tasks seem impossible—like looming mountains in your path -- and to climb them is almost too much to bear. Every day it is like this. Every day. The monotony of it leaves you wondering, what's the point?

As more attention is placed on mental health, the world learns a little more about how it is affected and by what. Twenty years ago, when I went to my doctors' appointments, no one asked if I was feeling depressed or if I ever wanted to hurt myself. Now, it's routine at every visit. *What took them so long? I guess its a start.* After the Columbine shooting in 1999, it seemed to me that mental health all of a sudden took front and center stage. *But they had to know that there was a problem, right? Why does it take something like this to happen for eyes to be opened?* That night on April 20, 1999, I wrote a song for those lost in that shooting. I titled it, "Is Heaven a Place in Your Heart?" It was a traumatic year for me. I was in my first year in college and that was when the anxiety and depression hit me head-on. It was like two freight trains carrying the weight of tons of cars colliding at high speeds.

A dark cloud loomed over me for many years. How does depression occur, you might ask? Well, I can only tell you what happened to me. Here it goes.

Traumatic childhood? Check. Living with an angry father who has an explosive temper kept me constantly on edge throughout my childhood. I thought, why can't he just be happy? Walking on eggshells became the norm at times for me, my mother, and my siblings. All that pent-up emotion had to come out sooner or later.

Loss of a loved one? Check. In eighth grade, I lost my friend unexpectedly. That morning when my friends and I arrived at school, we stood in the lobby and saw tears and disbelief on the faces of our classmates. We were told by another student that Rob had died in his sleep. The weight of that hit me like a cement block to the chest. We tried to use the payphone to call his house but no one remembered his home number. We had to be sure. But the faces confirmed it. *Gosh! What does death mean anyway? Why did he have to die? He was my friend. We were both only fourteen. I don't get it.* "Rob, why you teasin'?" He was always joking and smiling. "Aw, Maritza I'm just playin', you know I still love you." He laughed, his white teeth gleaming back at me. We were in science class. His final words to me echo in my mind as much today as they did that sad school morning when the thought hit me, I'd never see him again. To this day, I still don't understand why or how he passed.

Sickness? Check. *Will I ever get better? Is this fear going to finally kill me? Would that at least bring me peace? That's a comforting thought. Peace.*

Murder of innocent people? Check. *She was only fifteen. They said she was protecting her mother. Now I'm singing at her memorial service. Her sister and mother look so frail. I don't get it.* And then another friend of mine lost her sister in a terrible crime. *I can't believe she has to go through this. What if this happened to one of my sisters? I would go mad. I couldn't live with it. How do I be the friend she needs in this? Why God? I can't understand this. It's too much!*

And these are just some of the boxes I've checked.

Despite those dark times, I wanted to believe there was light up ahead. On my toughest days, I would tell myself to put one foot in front of the other and just do it. In college, there was this hill on campus I always had to climb, and it seemed to take forever to get to the top. *Just one-foot forward Maritza, don't worry about anything else. Walk. That's it. Now the other one, keep going.* Watching my feet, I quietly recited this until I finally reached the top. With my head down I hustled up that hill. My life with anxiety and depression was just that—a big hill, one right after another. Hustle after hustle. If I could move one foot forward, everything was going to be okay. At least, that's what I told myself.

I didn't believe it then, but I was building my strength in those trying moments. When I was depressed, it was hard to summon up the strength to get out of bed or even eat. My body felt like lead and my stomach was so agitated with nervousness, I was constantly nauseated. At times my depression felt like a deep black hole I could not escape.

But I am here to tell you that black holes did not swallow me. And I believe they won't for you as well. One step at a time, you can pass out of that tunnel to the end where the light is. I am not a therapist or educated in psychiatry—all I have is my experience. It all starts with a little faith.

I know there is a God out there because, in my lowest moments, He has come to me and brought me out of them. Again, and again, He has assured me my life matters and that I am loved. Each time suicidal thoughts loomed, and I was sure the end had come, He arrived right on time.

God loves us so completely, purely, and overwhelmingly that it may be easy to dismiss it altogether because it's unfathomable. We search away from God for quick fixes because the pain hurts so much, we desire immediate relief. It is hard to think that a loving God would allow this type of suffering. But the only thing that kept me going was my faith—that He knew my pain and cared enough to deliver me from the black holes in my life. He pulled me out of the darkness and into the light. I don't know how He did it. All I know is for many years I was stuck under a dark cloud, but now I am finally free under the sun, all because of Jesus Christ.

I am going to take you to the very beginning of when I started having symptoms of anxiety and depression. You will come to see how I made it to where I am now—a place of peace and deeper faith in God. Even though I still deal with some light, generalized anxiety and depression from time to time (Hello! This world is cray cray!), my life has turned out to be so much better than I had ever hoped, and I don't want to miss out on what else God has in store for me. This is my story.

Prologue

"It's here! Oh God, it's here!" I said aloud. I raced down the old road toward the steel building in my John Deere gator, pedal to the metal. I knew no matter how fast I drove; I would not escape it, I never could. "Let me get there, please! Just let me get there!"

I finally reached the old metal building where the construction office was for the Flight 93 Memorial Park in Shanksville, Pennsylvania. Pulling into the garage I shouted to my contractor who was in the office, "Gary! Gary!"

Gary Martin was my friend and the superintendent of the construction company that I worked with at the park. He rushed out of the office and seeing the pitiful state I was in, took action. I don't even remember what he said when he reached me. All I could tell him to do was one thing: "Hold me!" And he did.

The panic attack had arrived in full force and I knew I needed an anchor. He locked one hand onto my left shoulder and held me firm as the attack racked my body. I began to vomit uncontrollably. I could no longer process my senses—hearing, smell, and taste were muted, gone. But sight and touch were intensified. All I could do was vomit liquid onto the floor of my gator. My body flapped like a rag doll from the convulsions. I could not stop it or control it. His firm grip on me held me sure because there was no way I could get through it on my own strength. Adrenalin coursed through my veins like molten lava. My skin was ultra-sensitized so that the light wind on that Pennsylvania mountaintop felt like a thousand needles sticking me at once.

My mind was a blur. All I could do was focus on the floor of the gator where my insides surrendered all that was in me, waiting for the attack to end. Finally, it released some of its hold on me. I was spent. Gary helped me out of the gator and into a chair in his office where I let my body slump and my arms fall to my sides. Fitz, the quality control manager for the construction of the park, was also present and began to clean my gator with a hose outside. I had no strength left and felt like rubber. Then the urge came to go to the bathroom and finish from the other end. I didn't think I could do it. I felt that I would go right there and then, and the fear came again. Yet somehow, I mustered up whatever strength was left in me and I made it to the toilet.

Afterward, completely drained, I slowly returned to the chair. I asked Gary to call Laura to take me home to the farm. The attack was over for now and I needed to return to my comfort zone and recharge. Sitting in that chair, one question loomed in my mind. Would I turn left and allow this attack to sink me into depression again...or would I turn right for a change?

Chapter One
Beginnings

Comparing myself to others was the catalyst for my depression and anxiety. It made me self-conscious, which led to low self-esteem. It always stole my joy. It was so constant—it became routine in my life. It is still easy to give into it at times if I allow myself. It is a hard habit to break, but not unbreakable.

The first person I compared myself to at five years old was my friend Sasha. I found myself lacking. We lived on base in the city of El Paso, Texas. Our parents served in the United States Army there. Sasha lived across the street from us, and we played together often. I remember her having brown hair and light eyes. She was very sweet, and I enjoyed playing together. One day, Mami was having a conversation with Sasha's mother. I heard her say that Sasha had a nice shape and that she would have an attractive figure when she was grown. I was always listening in on Mami's conversations with other adults despite her telling me not to. I wonder now if I had heeded her advice, and not heard that comment about Sasha, would I have compared myself to her? Maybe my story would have started differently, maybe not.

Sasha had shapely hips and a well-rounded rear-end for a young girl. I instantly became jealous of this, and in my mind, my skinny, bony shape was not enough. She had something I didn't, and it didn't matter that Mami would compliment me too.

"Mami, am I pretty too? Is my figure nice too?"

"Yes Maritza, you are very pretty and have a nice figure. I keep telling you but you don't listen."

It didn't matter to me because I was looking at Sasha, and as far as I was concerned, she was better than me.

Reflecting on this in later years, I realized that at the time, Mami was probably too young to know how her comments might have made me feel. I don't believe she said the things she did to make me feel bad. She was just saying them as innocent observations, the way women do when they talk with each other. But whatever the reason, from that point on, I would struggle with comparing my figure to those of other girls.

I admired other girls' calves because I didn't have any. My legs were so skinny, they looked like sticks. I never liked to wear shorts or bathing suits because I would be too embarrassed. I didn't have shapely hips like other girls either, so I hated that as well. I was constantly looking at other girls' bodies and comparing myself to them throughout elementary, middle, and high school, and eventually college.

In my middle school years, when everyone is introduced to gym class and locker rooms, I would notice how the girls' clothing fit their bodies, conscious of my own body and how my clothes fit me. In the locker room, I would change quickly hoping no one would notice my rail-thin figure all the while I was noticing others. As the girls' laughter and talk filled the locker room, I would observe how nice their hair was styled and I'd become frustrated with my hair coming out of place and looking frizzy as I hastily pulled my shirt over my head. I felt unkempt and less put together than they were even though I'd taken the time to look nice before I left for school each day. I would see how their hips would fill out their shorts and their fully shaved and moisturized calves would end at neat socks and popular sneakers. No matter how often I shaved my legs it seemed it was not enough as I always had stubble, and with my hair being so dark, it was easily seen. I thought I had no hips, a small butt, and no calves compared to them. This made me feel less feminine, incomplete, and very sad. It wasn't like this every day at school, but the thoughts were not far from my mind. Not only was it exhausting, it was also very depressing. The beauty standards of the world didn't help either.

I was also unmercifully made fun of for my hair in middle school. It was thick, frizzy, and very dry, so it stuck up. Gel and hairspray were used a lot during the early nineties and those products were horrible for my hair. All they did was dry it out more. Later in life, I found moisturizing products for my type of hair and learned all I needed was good hydration to get the curly look I wanted. The girls at school would perm their hair straight and use gel or "grease" to slick it back. The natural styles of today would have been made fun of back then.

Not only would the girls make fun of my hair, but the guys would also tend to give me hair tips as if trying to help. One kid told me all I needed was a perm and I'd "be good." He said something like, "you got good hair so you just need a perm and you would be good." I murmured back something like "yeah" but in my mind, I never wanted to get a perm because I knew if I did, it would damage and burn my hair and make it frizzier. I knew they wouldn't understand so at times I didn't explain all that. Though they figured they were trying to help, it just solidified my dislike for my hair even more.

The kids would humiliate me by calling me names like "Bush" because they thought my hair looked like one. Even the guy I had a crush on made fun of me. Sometimes, I would catch my friends laughing at what the other kids said about me, and since I was such a people-pleaser, I didn't fault my friends although it hurt me deeply. One time in seventh grade Mami let her friend who was training at a salon school cut my hair. She cut it into a curly mullet. A MULLET! I didn't know until I saw myself in the mirror afterward. Since my hair was dry and very curly, the shorter it was, the curlier it got. Without proper hydration, the curls turned to frizzy strands that I had difficulty taming. This new haircut gave me more to deal with on top of all my other struggles. When I went to the bathroom after she was done and saw myself, I cried. I hated it. I knew what was coming when I returned to school.

That was a holiday weekend, so we didn't get back to school until Wednesday of the next week. I wanted my friend to see my hair before going to school so that she could give it to me straight. *If Trina can see me, she would be real with me. Maybe my hair isn't that bad. Could I be wrong?* We weren't able to meet up until school began. Finally, at school, Trina and another friend of mine looked at me and I could see it on their faces. Trina tried to be kind but her facial expression revealed what her words did not. She frowned, scrunching her face in disdain. "It's not that.... bad."

"I know guys, I know. It sucks." During the morning I just went with it and headed to class. Then came lunch period. I remember walking down the hall with my friends and classmates to lunch and a couple of girls, who were my constant bullies, began laughing so hard they were bent over holding their knees. I wasn't sure at first what they were laughing at until I realized... it was me.

I didn't want to go to school anymore because of the bullying. I wanted the whole seventh-grade year to be over already. I had dreams that my hair had grown back to normal. It was a constant thought. Not only was I self-conscious about my body and hair, but this new haircut made it worse. I didn't feel pretty. I felt ugly.

Mami was very apologetic. And being the person I have always been, I understood and believed she was just trying to help. I got through it, nonetheless.

High school was a bit more forgiving, surprisingly. I remember wearing a nice red dress to school that was form-fitting hoping that it would accentuate my figure. I heard a boy say "Darn!" as I passed by and I hoped he meant that for me as a compliment. Later that same day a friend of mine told me that I had a small butt. It made me feel like I couldn't fill out that dress and reluctantly, I agreed with her. I still compared myself to others and felt inadequate. I was "skinny," and they were "shapely." When I looked at myself in the mirror, I saw a girl with so much hair and a small body. I joked that my hair took all the nutrients and my body got the leftovers. I convinced myself for a short time I wanted to be fat because being skinny was not healthy and being fat was!

It's funny how those kids that gave me a hard time in school ended up being my friends in my later school years and in life. I believe that was God. Today, people love my hair. They say that most people go to the salons to get what I have naturally. Nevertheless, there are still times when I have a hard time accepting the way my hair is. Then, I fix it nice and think, Wow! Thank You, God, for my hair! What a turnaround! I wish I would have fixed it like this back in school!

Today, I believe bullying made me stronger, although I would never want anyone to feel the way I did back then nor do I condone it. To me, I was this very skinny girl with all this hair. I used to joke that I was an upside-down mop, a wad of hair, and a rail-thin body. I realize now our words have power and I shouldn't have joked about myself in such a way. But I was a kid, what did I know?

I am the oldest of five kids and we are of Puerto Rican descent, born and raised in the United States. Papi was born in Puerto

Rico and Mami was born in the Bronx, New York. Both were born to Puerto Rican parents. They met in college, got married, and started their family.

I have two younger brothers and two younger sisters. My brothers, Ezra and Joshua, are tall and handsome. Ezra is darker in complexion and Joshua is fairer. Both are very funny and have a zest for travel. They are airmen in the United States Air Force serving our country overseas, taking after Papi who served in the Army for almost twenty years. I always enjoy hearing about all the places they have visited with their jobs. From the United States to Europe, Asia to Africa, and the Middle East, they have seen the world and I am so proud of them. My sisters Mary and Ariana are also tall and are fashionistas. I have always admired how they can put together outfits and accessorize them with the few pieces of costume jewelry that we had.

Mary was good at fixing her hair—whether she wore it curly or straight, she made it look effortless. When she wears her hair curly, she looks like an exotic Persian princess with her long, dark brown shiny ringlets. Her complexion is dark, similar to Ezra's.

Ariana is fair with long, straight brown hair. Ariana is very good at applying makeup. She knows about all the right face creams to use and applies color artfully and effortlessly. I have always thought they were both very beautiful and talented.

I am in the middle of their dark and fair complexions. My hair is closer to Mary's in texture and length. When we wore our hair curly, people would comment that we were twins although she has fewer frizzies than I do. I would jokingly say that I looked like a bag lady while my sisters were always so pretty. Mary would tell me not to say that about myself—all I needed to do was invest in myself a little more.

Since we were a military family, we grew up living in various places. We lived in Texas for a while, then Germany, Maryland, Washington, and Maryland again. However, that's the part of my childhood that I wouldn't change. I enjoyed experiencing different places and meeting different people.

When Papi joined the army, I was just two years old. We were living in the Bronx, New York and Ezra had just been born.

When I was young, I remember feeling like I couldn't wait to grow up because of all the fighting in our house. Papi was always fighting with Mami and us kids. Sometimes his anger was valid, like the times when we kids did not pick up after ourselves but most times it wasn't. There were times I'd stand in the middle of Papi and my brothers and even between my parents when the bickering would start. I would be shaking with fear that the argument would get out of hand and turn physical.

Chapter Two
Mami and Papi

The first time Mami left Papi was when I was about five years old when we were living in El Paso. The way I heard it, Mami thought Papi was having an affair. I watched her fold our clothes in the living room and pack them into a large box. Before I knew it, the four of us kids (Ariana had not yet been born) and thirteen pieces of luggage were crammed into the family Chevrolet Chevette and headed out of El Paso. We were on our way to her hometown in New York, where my grandparents awaited us.

We didn't make it very far because the money began to run out, only getting us into Arkansas. The night before we turned around, Mami spoke to Papi over the phone in our motel room. He convinced her that he had never betrayed her and the next morning we headed back home.

"Now when we get back home, I want you guys to tell your father that he is the best daddy in the whole world," she said.

When we arrived, I did just that as he pulled the luggage out of the car. "Mami told us to tell you that you are the best daddy in the whole world." Yes, I said every word. Papi smiled in return, but I thought I sensed a hint of sadness in his eyes.

Even though I was very young at the time, I felt like the trip had been an exciting adventure, looking out the window at the scenery and sleeping in motel rooms at night. Now, as an adult, I realize how brave Mami was to have left him with four kids under the age of six in tow. Her bravery and boldness would continue to amaze me throughout my life and provide the strength and assurance I needed.

I have always thought of myself as being wise because as the oldest, I had to look after my brothers and sisters while I was growing up. I felt more like an adult than a kid back then. Mami used to get mad at me and tell me to go hang out with kids my age, but I didn't always want to. I'd rather listen to the adults talk.

I found myself somehow understanding grown folk's problems and issues. Their conversations were always more entertaining and interesting than those of young kids. I felt that I could relate, being the eldest and having responsibilities, as if I was a young mother myself. While Mami and Papi were at work, I was left in charge of my siblings after school. It was like I had four kids sometimes. Mami used to say I had an old soul. I guess she was right because I felt older than I was.

Mami was a very big part of our childhood, but she had to work along with Papi to support such a large family. Since the age of nine, I performed some of the daily caretaking. And since my parents could trust me, it was easier for them to lean on me at times. I didn't always mind it.

Because Papi was in the US Army, Mami would have to find jobs wherever we were stationed. She worked several jobs throughout my childhood and all of them changed due to us moving around. While living in Germany, she worked in the mess hall of a military hospital. When we moved to Maryland, she worked cleaning buildings on the Proving Grounds. She worked there on weekends and Papi worked during the week while we went to school. Sometimes I would go and help Mami work on the weekends. While we worked together, the rest of my siblings would be at home with Papi. Being with her at her job was also an escape from his anger.

Some weekends she would take me to her cleaning job and afterward, we would get fast food from McDonald's. I liked that mostly because we could relax and enjoy lunch together, just me and Mami. It was our quality time.

I also learned the importance of manual labor and the humility that comes with it. Cleaning up after others made me think twice about leaving a mess for someone else to clean up. For instance, every time my sisters and I eat at a restaurant, we empty the plates and stack them together with the utensils on top, and put all the paper trash over them. This way the server can pick every bit of it up in one swoop. Thoughtfulness matters and I learned it from Mami being in service to others.

Another job Mami had was as the military post operator on the base where we lived. I could call her anytime; like when my brothers were fighting or not listening to me. I'm sure she wasn't so keen on receiving my calls!

In Germany, Ezra, Joshua, and I all went to school together. I made sure that my siblings and I sat together on the bus to school so I could protect them. I sat on the outside with both Joshua and Ezra sitting on the inside. Our first day on the bus an older female student came to us and nicely said that only two were allowed to a seat, yet she indicated that we could stay the way we were for the rest of the ride home. Moving forward, that would have to change. I looked up at her and felt embarrassed but said, okay. The three of us stayed together in the seat all the way home that day. Over time we made friends and were comfortable sitting with them.

One tortuous afternoon when it was time to get on the bus and head home, my brother Ezra missed it. Mami wanted us to take a different bus home and although two went to the apartments in which we lived, one stopped further away than the other. The buses were numbered 23 & 29. We normally took bus 23 because it left us at the top of the hill, closer to home. Bus 29 left us further down the hill. I didn't feel comfortable taking bus 29 this time because I wasn't crazy about change, and I worried about it. Ezra seemed worried too. At the end of the school day, I found bus 29 easily and waited for Ezra. After a while, when all the kids emptied the schoolyard, the buses began to slowly pull off. I was standing up in the seat desperately searching for my little brother. From the window inside the bus, I saw him walking along the school building very slowly looking defeated and scared. I wanted to yell out "halt" to the German bus driver for him to stop so I could call my brother over—but I didn't. I just watched as we slowly drove away from him. I felt wretched!

My friends tried to console me saying that we could borrow Mami's friend's car to go back and get Ezra. The only car we had at the time was with Papi at work.

To this day, I hate that I didn't ask the bus driver to stop for him. When I got off the bus at the bottom of the hill, Mami was there. She asked where Ezra was. I told her he missed the bus. "What? What do you mean he missed the bus?" I saw her face fill with worry and fear and we began to walk up the hill very fast to our apartment. I could see the worry transfer to her body as she kept her arms crossed tightly at her chest. I asked if we could borrow a friend's car to go get him. I don't remember her exact words but she indicated that was not an option. My heart sank. How are we going to get him now? I thought. I was angry at Mami for making us take another bus. Why did she have to change it? We were comfortable taking bus 23. As I think on it now, being from New York City, Mami always had to know of alternate routes to get home. It was the street smarts in her. I guess she was trying to teach us a little bit of that—not getting too comfortable using one way.

Mami's worrying increased because Ezra had to wait at school until Papi was done working at five o'clock to pick him up. I was racked with guilt and worry. Finally, at the end of the day, Ezra came home with Papi. I was so relieved!

Ezra was in first grade and I was in second. Although we were both fairly young, I was responsible for him and I knew better. That evening I stood at the entrance to my parents' bedroom feeling like a failure, watching Mami hold him tightly in her arms as she cried silently. He still had his little backpack on. I could feel her relief that he was home safe, but I could also feel her fear and sadness too. Papi was looking at them and I could see the sadness in his face too as he watched Mami cry. He never liked to see her cry—none of us did. The guilt washed over me like a bucket of dirty, cold water. I had let them all down.

I carry that memory with me every year of my life. I know Ezra doesn't care anymore and I doubt he even remembers, but I do.

I decided to finally forgive myself and let it go after hearing a homily in church about pride. I thought that I had always been good at not having a problem with pride and that I worked hard to remain humble because if I had any pride, I would be like Papi and suffer for it.

The pastor that Sunday spoke about pride and forgiveness. He explained that when we feel we have done something too bad for God to forgive and think we can never be forgiven, it's a sign of pride. Nothing is too big if the person is seeking God's forgiveness, he explained. I just needed to ask for forgiveness and let it go. But it wasn't as easy as it sounded. I did ask for God's forgiveness for not speaking up and telling the bus driver to stop for my little brother, but it wasn't until I forgave myself that I could finally let it go. I realized God never held my actions against me. He wanted me to release myself from the prison of guilt. After all, I was just a kid.

Mami never expected me to assume the role of secondary mother, I just took it upon myself to be there for my siblings. At two years old, she showed me how to hold the bottle and feed Ezra. I was pretty curious about him, the way young kids are about new babies, and I wanted to help. It probably kept me out of trouble, too. Nothing keeps a little kid out of mischief more than giving him or her something "grown-up" to do!

At five years old, before we started taking the bus the next year, Ezra and I walked home by ourselves from school while Mami took care of Joshua and Mary who were babies at the time. Times were different than they are now. Nobody ever dreamed about school shootings. We were safer back then I think.

At nine years old, I was the one with the key to get us inside after school, making sure we all walked together and remained home until Mami and Papi came from work. We did have a before and after school babysitter at the apartment complex where we lived, a friend of my Mami's. She would check in on us when we came home each day, but I made sure we all got home okay.

I allowed the kids to go outside for a while to play after school. Even when I played with my friends, I would keep one eye on my siblings. Joshua and Ezra didn't particularly like the idea of me being in charge of them. Of course, being boys, they gave me problems at times, but most of the time, I was able to keep them in line, and more importantly, safe. Because of the help I provided in looking after my siblings, I gained more of my parents' respect. I treasured that very much as a young child because it gave me confidence.

We were first stationed in Fort Hood, TX, where Joshua was born and then moved to Fort Bliss, TX. We lived on base and one of my memories was of Joshua always being adventurous and getting lost when we were little. He would wander off by himself and it would scare Mami. At age twenty-five, Mami had four children under the age of five and was over a thousand miles away from family and friends. While Papi worked during the day, she had to deal with all us kids, running around and keeping count of us. She took us everywhere she went because she didn't have anyone with whom she could leave us.

Well, it was one of those busy days when Joshua escaped her watch and got lost. When she found out, she walked up and down the street crying out his name as the tears fell. I was on my bike outside and one of my friends asked me, "Is that your mom?" "Yes," I said with embarrassment. This wasn't the first time.

Joshua also had a problem with sleepwalking and would leave the house early in the morning or in the middle of the night. One night, Mami awoke to find the front door open. She knew he had left again. She ran out looking for him and finally found him in his diaper, with no clothes on, asleep in someone's backyard. Even though we were living in hot El Paso, the nights did get chilly. God protected him and I am forever grateful for it. It could have been a lot worse.

Being very close to Mami, I tended to feel what she felt. I worried when she worried. I cried when she cried. I was happy when she was, and so on. I cared how she felt. I was always sympathetic with others, to the point where I started to be an obsessive "people-pleaser," who always put the needs or desires of others before my own.

One night while we were still living in El Paso, Papi came home drunk. We kids were in our rooms asleep but I woke to the sounds of him kicking things in the house and could hear Mami pleading with him to stop yelling. He continued kicking at the blinds and the window, slamming the counter tops and cabinets with his hands and feet, and cursing and yelling at God to speak to him.

That night, I thought the Devil was coming for my dad. I thought if there was one thing that was forbidden, it was to curse at God. I was always afraid to question God or even be angry at Him. I was taught He would punish you, although I know now that we punish ourselves.

Papi broke a few things that night with his thrashing and kicking. The military police came to our house, and all of a sudden, he behaved like a boy scout. That was the only time I had ever heard Papi call out to God. I was around six years old at the time and it was terrifying. Today I can look back and see how it was a natural thing to do—Papi was crying out to God in desperation—but to a little kid it felt very scary.

Chapter Three
Abuelita

Spirituality was very hard to experience in my house growing up. Papi did not go to church, and Mami was a practicing Catholic. She worked hard to make sure we received all the Sacraments. We all had our baptisms, communions, and confirmations. Papi didn't get in the way of her rearing us in the Church, but he did not make it easy either. He constantly complained to her about the hypocrisy in the Church, which was one of the reasons he didn't go.

Despite all his complaining and badgering, Mami still followed through with the practices of our faith. He thought we were fools to think that religion or church could save us. When he started his rants on religion, no one could escape—we just had to wait for him to finish. "...and what is all this Hallelujah capituyah singing?" he'd rant sarcastically. "People say one thing in Church then say and do another outside. Hypocrites! I can't stand it!" Oh gosh, will he ever stop? Isn't this blasphemy? Isn't he tired of repeating the same things over and over? Does he think we want to keep hearing this? Always the same rant. I was so tired of his tirades. During my entire childhood and much of my adult life, he would carry on the same argument. No one could say anything because he would only raise his voice and get even more impossible. His hatred for the Catholic Church caused a great divide between my parents.

The first person who influenced my faith was my maternal grandmother, Abuelita, who helped raise me in my first year while Mami and Papi were at college. Abuelita was around five feet tall but would become shorter over the years. Her white and black hair was like mine in that it would stick up too but was silkier. She had skin coloring like that of coffee with cream and her wrinkles told of years of laughter and tears. This thin little lady that everyone loved had such power in her stance that for me, I felt closer to God being just next to her. That power came from the love she had for her family and for Jesus Christ. She never used it to hurt anyone, only to shower love on everyone she met. Everyone in the projects back in the Bronx, called her "Mami" because she was a mother to so many. She had such an aura of gentleness and faith that many people were drawn to her. And despite Papi's lack of faith and love for the Church, he was even softened by her presence and wouldn't argue with her. He loved her and my grandfather very much.

Abuelita grew up in a convent in San Juan, Puerto Rico. Her mother died young giving birth, and her father, a very poor man, couldn't raise all nine children on his own so he sent her to live there. I guess he believed she would be safe there. It was in the convent with the nuns that Abuelita developed a deep love for Christ. It was that love that made me love Christ as well.

She didn't speak English very well and neither did my grandfather, Papi Chi, Mami's father, so Abuelita taught me how to speak Spanish and pray to God. While stationed in Maryland, we visited New York occasionally on the weekends since it was a three-hour ride. We would drive up on Fridays after my parents got out of work and return after church on Sundays. Many times, we would go to Long Island to visit my aunt and cousins on Papi's side then come home to Maryland on Sundays. Abuelita and Papi Chi lived on the fourteenth floor of a brick building that was part of the Bronx River Projects in New York. It is where Mami was raised with her four brothers. When we visited Abuelita, she would always greet us by waving out of her kitchen window fourteen stories up. After getting off the elevator (if it was working, if not, we walked fourteen flights of stairs!) she would be there with the door open and eager to give us one of her loving hugs, raining kisses on us. We would each get tons of kisses with a blessing and an "I love you." Her greetings were so full of love, excitement, and joy that they made you feel special, and you never wanted to leave. At least I didn't.

The small three-bedroom, single-bathroom apartment would smell of sofrito (a cooking base made of vegetables we use for our rice), rice, and chicken. The thick aroma would make my stomach grumble and my mouth water. Then she'd feed us dinner and we would catch up, talk about telenovelas (Spanish for soap operas), how the family was, and God. She took me to the noon Mass with her on those Sundays if we didn't go to Long Island, and I would sing with her in the choir. She would always fix my hair nicely, doing hot oil treatments and putting in rollers. She explained that my type of hair needed a lot of tender love and care and when she was done, I'd always feel so beautiful. My hair was different in her hands. She knew how to handle it. It was too much for me, and Mami never really learned how to fix my hair, so it was a treat when Abuelita would do it. There is a picture of her washing her hair and bathing me in her kitchen sink when I was around a year old. I am smiling up at the camera, soapy suds in my hair and she is smiling down at me. She knew my struggle with my hair and thus always did her best to make me feel pretty and special.

I loved to hear her sing church songs while doing her chores or combing my hair. She had such a sweet voice and I believe my musical ability came from her. Papi's side of the family is very musical as well, but I was raised singing with Abuelita. When I sing in my church choir today, especially when we sing songs I recall from my youth, I am reminded of my time with her, and I still feel connected to her. Sometimes, I can still hear her singing as if she's in the choir with me again, and the tears threaten to fall.

I think Abuelita always felt closer to me because I was the first grandchild, and I made an effort to try to communicate with her. Also, I think I was special to her because I tried to be like her. When we visited, I was always at her side. I followed her around like a puppy and would listen in on her conversations with Mami. I loved it when she would tuck us in and then pray. I loved the attention she would give me, and I think she loved the attention I gave her. No matter what was going on, I wanted to be her pride and joy.

One summer I stayed in New York with her, and we had a blast. We didn't do anything or go anywhere particularly special, just being together made us both so happy. It was easy to be close to her. When at last, it was time to go back home to Maryland, my Uncle Angel, one of Mami's brothers, drove us all back and they stayed to visit us.

When it was time for my grandparents to return to New York, I had the hardest time saying goodbye to Abuelita. We held each other and cried that last morning of her visit. She told me that although we had our special time, not to forget Mami who was missing my affection all the while I was giving it to Abuelita. I had become so close to her; I forgot my own mother.

"Little one, when I leave, I want you to go to your mother. She needs you. Tell her you love her. Remember, I am only your grandmother. She is your mother. Don't forget that my love," she said as she gently stroked my hair.

"Okay, Abuelita, I will." I cried silently. I watched her get into Uncle Angel's gray Cadillac and look up at me through the window, tears in her eyes too as she waved goodbye, and they drove off.

When Mami came home that day from work, I went to her. "Mami, I'm sorry that I forgot you. You are my mother and I love you very much!" Falling into her arms on the couch, she held me and cried too. I'd never meant to ignore her. Abuelita's presence was so strong, I just wanted to be in it always. I am grateful my relationship with my grandmother was so special.

As much as she spoke about love and God, Abuelita was pretty good about instilling fear too, even though her intentions were pure. She would warn me about how the world was getting worse and that I always needed to keep my eyes open. This kind of talk allowed fear to grow in me. Papi was the same way.

She also gave me a skewed view of sex. She would say if anyone touched me down there it was bad and kissing with the tongue was bad. She didn't have any sexual experiences other than those with my grandfather. Sex before marriage was a sin. Any touching before marriage was also a sin, so I grew up thinking all boys were "fresh" and only wanted sex. Well, I didn't want anything to do with that. I was told to always protect myself and my body from such things.

When I started to have physical desires for sex, I felt guilty and fearful of going to hell just for thinking about it. I thought Abuelita would not understand my inner conflict. Despite my shame, the thoughts about sex would continue to occupy my mind. Sex was everywhere, in music, on TV, and at school where many of the students were engaging in it. Remembering what Abuelita said, and feeling that boys were only looking for sex, made me want to become a nun!

I resolved at eighteen years old that I wasn't going to allow sex to pull me down into an inescapable desire that would lead me straight to hell—I was going to consecrate myself and devote my body and life to God. I went so far as to investigate what it would take to become a nun, but I stopped when Mami reminded me that one day I would want a family of my own. She cautioned me to consider how hard it would be to surrender my dreams of a family, even though a nun's life was also rewarding. I thought about one day, looking into the eyes of a child, my child. I decided that becoming a nun was not my path.

To be honest, what Abuelita said about sex did help me, though. I learned to respect my body because it was a gift from God and His temple. When I think about it now, it wasn't all bad. She was teaching the way she was taught—that sex is something sacred and created to be such by God. It is the way we get to partner with Him in creating life and enjoying it. He gave us that and He is good and holy. So, I eventually reasoned, shouldn't sex be holy too?

Chapter Four
Family Feud

I used to hate those early nineties family TV shows, that inaccurately portrayed what went on in families like mine. (But I still watched them!) Had we been put on TV we probably could have made millions! America loves all the fighting and cursing. Just look at reality shows. It's not interesting unless there's major conflict. Sadly, it always seems to draw the most attention. Put two women fighting on TV, and it will get more views than any show having to do with God or decency.

But I couldn't relate to most of those shows because I felt like those father figures weren't real. I couldn't imagine any father being so understanding with their children, not giving them spankings or cursing at them. Maybe I was just angry because those fathers depicted a way of loving that I didn't have. Real life was rough, and I couldn't wait to grow up and get out of the house.

It didn't help that Papi had depression issues of his own. He was always hanging out with his friends instead of being with us. I think it was an escape for him—from the reality at home.

One sunny morning, while we were still living in El Paso, Texas, Papi and Mami argued and he stormed out of the house. We were all supposed to go to the store but we only had one car. He got in the car and left us at home.

I stood outside with Mami in our driveway watching him drive back and forth on the main road in front of our house. As he drove by each time, he gave her this pitiful look as we continued to wait for him in our driveway. It made me wonder, What's wrong with us? Why is he doing this? Why can't he just come pick us up?

We went back into the house, and I knew Mami was very angry. To get back at him she threw his army uniform on the floor and poured baby powder on it, and she began to stomp on it laughing. As a little kid, I joined her in the fun. In the military, a soldier's uniform is his identity and is very important. It must remain cleaned and pressed. A soldier must always be sharp in her/his attire. I guess Mami really wanted to show him how she felt. But I believe she did it mostly because she was deeply hurt and felt defeated. She couldn't depend on him and there was no one else. My heart went out to her. I was six at the time but seemed to understand her frustration and hurt. I don't remember us ever making it to the store that day.

When he was home, most of the time Papi's temper was so bad we wanted him to go to his friend's house and stay for as long as he desired. Many times, that was exactly what he did and it was a reprieve for all of us.

As I grew and began to better understand my people-pleasing issues, I realized Papi was also a people-pleaser. In my opinion, he seemed to do more for his friends and their families than he did for us. I think he felt tied down with us and never really felt like he lived. I don't think there was ever anyone with whom Papi could talk, and, if ever there was, he probably didn't want to go down that road. Papi could be a very angry, depressed, and negative person. Maybe it was partly the way he grew up and partly the old-fashioned Latino culture. Latinos usually rear their children with guilt and fear. The way I experienced it, fear was used as a method to keep children from doing wrong—there would be a warning of a consequence like a spanking or a beating. Another disciplinary tactic used was instilling guilt. The rationale was if you could be made to feel guilty enough for what you did you wouldn't do it again. I often felt guilty, and now believe that is how Papi felt, too. We just acted out in different ways.

Today, I believe a lot of families use these tactics, not just Latino families. I hear about how some of my friends grew up and the disciplinary actions they faced were similar to mine. Raising a family in this world is very hard and as they say, there is no instruction manual for it. I think people just do the best they can with what they know. This by no means justifies any abuse that comes from discipline or punishments.

Growing up, if anyone tried to make Papi feel guilty, the beast would rear its ugly head and roar, and would even fight if it felt threatened…even by his own sons. The general rule was, Papi was to be respected and obeyed even if it meant we disagreed.

There were times Papi and my brothers would fight with each other, and I was always in the midst of the fray trying to stop it. One never knew what mood Papi would be in, which is why I would get so furious with my brothers for instigating fight after fight. They knew Papi would blow up if they came home late or spent too much time in the bathroom. I figured if you left Papi alone, followed his rules, and stayed out of his way, the household would be more peaceful. Then again, there were times when nobody did anything wrong and he would still be angry. Go figure.

Most of the time at home my siblings and I tried not to give Papi a reason to fight by making sure everything was in order or everyone was accounted for. He didn't want us to go outside and play much, opting to have us stay in the house so he wouldn't have to be bothered with watching us outside. He said he wanted to protect us, but I felt that as long as we were in the house we couldn't get into trouble and that was all he wanted.

When Papi fought with the boys, I feared one of them would get badly injured. He was so filled with anger, I didn't know how far he would go. There were times when it was hard to sleep for fear that the fighting would start again. I remember Mami screaming at Papi and pleading with him to stop fighting with the boys because she was also afraid.

One night, a huge brawl occurred between Papi and the boys in Ezra's room. We were living in Washington state at the time. I cannot remember what started it but when it ended, they were all separated. Everyone went to their rooms except me. I went to sleep on the floor of my parents' bedroom. Shaking from the aftereffects of the fighting, I breathed in the cold air that entered at the base of the bedroom door. I lay there watching my brothers' room from across the hall, making sure they were safe. I had placed myself in between Papi and the boys as a human shield to protect them. I always felt I had to make sure no other fighting would take place— as if I was physically strong enough to keep three males apart!

I was eighteen years old, five-foot-four inches tall, and weighed only ninety-eight pounds. There was no way that I would be able to stop any physical fighting between my brothers and Papi. Still, I was ready and willing to jump in if needed. I thought if I could scream and shake enough, my pitiful state would draw their attention back to me and stop the fighting. Later, I learned that this tactic I'd invented through my fears would cause the fiercest of my panic attacks.

It's clear that while growing up, fear was something I struggled with from early on. It was unfathomable for me to think that I couldn't be there when the fighting started because I had to make sure we all lived through it. It was vital to me to be present when things got out of control at home.

Despite the fights with my brothers, Papi didn't like to spank us girls. It seemed like the boys were always getting spanked when we were little. As soon as Papi would raise his voice, the anxiety in me would also rise. How far would it go today?

"Whose socks are these? Joshua! Get out of the shower! Do you pay the bills? Where the h*** are my keys?" he would yell. And so on and so on.

It didn't matter what made him angry. He seemed to have an insurmountable amount of angry energy inside of him. I don't think he knew how to handle it. He knew he had a problem with it because he would try to justify it when fighting.

"You guys just don't learn! And you wonder why Papi gets so angry. I am not a happy camper right now!"

I hated when he said that. It sounds funny to someone who doesn't hear that saying much, but we heard it all the time, and it wasn't funny to us. That saying annoyed me more than any other because we weren't happy campers either! I don't believe we were particularly bad kids. When I think about it now, as an adult, I can sometimes see that what Papi did at the time was what he thought was best. However, it doesn't excuse his behavior. Maybe that was all he knew. Dealing with such anger must not have been easy for him. Maybe he felt insecure, or he was grappling with something inside. Even with all that he still provided for us, he never abandoned us, and interestingly he could be as affectionate as he was angry. I would find out later in life through conversations with my aunts that as a child, Papi had rough times as well.

The oldest of eight children born to both his parents (I say this because he has other siblings that share the same father), Papi was responsible for his siblings just as I felt I was. I heard tales from my aunts of the spankings he would get during his childhood. I figured the way he treated us was the only way he knew to raise and discipline children.

It also didn't help that he was in the army. After he was done lecturing us, he'd tell us we were "dismissed." But we weren't soldiers in the Army, young recruits to be whipped into shape. We were just kids. His lectures felt like a form of emotional abuse because they would often leave us, or me, feeling stupid.

One afternoon, Papi summoned me to the living room. He always calls me by my nickname.

"Maricita," he called in a stern and firm tone.

"What?" I answered back. Bad move.

"Don't say 'what,' that's wrong!" He barked. "When I call you, reply with 'yes sir!' Now go and wash the dishes. You're dismissed."

I turned around and headed for the kitchen. He was right, I shouldn't have answered with 'what?' But the 'yes sir' and 'you're dismissed' and his tone seemed a bit much and irritated me. Just another one of those days, I guess.

When Papi was affectionate it created a complicated feeling in me because I couldn't fake my dislike for the other ways he treated us. After a fight, he would always come and give us kisses and hugs. I hated that because I'd still be fuming about the punishment, and it wasn't easy to turn off that emotion and exchange it for a happier one. My family on Papi's side is very affectionate. They give hugs and kisses all the time and are constantly saying "God bless you." But all of that was hard to take when I didn't particularly feel close to him because of the way he was in his anger. Therefore, signs of affection on my part for him were few.

He often noticed this and would even say sarcastic things which made it harder to be affectionate toward him. "What's the matter, you can't kiss and hug your father?" he would ask, his tone rising. I really didn't want to but if I refused there would be more fighting, so I would go and hug him and tell him I loved him. Walking away, feelings of irritation and annoyance filled my heart. I guess if he never asked, I may not have shown any affection towards him and maybe he knew that.

I do remember one fun family vacation we had. While living in Germany in 1989, we visited Berlin as the Wall was coming down. During the trip up to Berlin, Papi took a break from driving and let Mami drive. He then came to the back of our van where we were and began playing with us. He took our Fraggle Rock stuffed animals and made them dance and it was quite funny. We laughed and saw a kinder, more fun side to him. It was a rare treat to see him engaging with us and having fun doing it. We would catch glimpses of his happy side over the years, but they became fewer and fewer as we grew up. When we finally arrived in Berlin, Papi and Mami encountered a problem with our hotel room. The problem was, there was no hotel room! After many hours of driving, this was not what my parents wanted to hear. I guess the hotel gave away our room or something happened because we had to sleep in the van that night.

There was about two or three feet of snow outside and it was still coming down. Mami and us kids went to sleep in the makeshift bed that was at the back of the van. I awoke to Mami arguing with Papi because he fell asleep with the heater on. The next morning, I had to go to the bathroom, and guess where I went? In the snow. With my bare behind in the freezing cold, I peed in the snow just outside the van because we didn't have a bathroom to use.

We were able to get a room later that day. Walking into the hotel, the lobby was huge. The décor was very old, and the red carpet was dingy. The red color reminded me of the Russian flag.

The carpet seemed to fill the entire lobby that appeared big enough for a small country to fit in. The windows were large and almost seemed to touch the ceiling and floor. It may not have actually been so grand, but everything seems large to a little kid. As big as the place was, there was an old feel to it—as if it had been around for centuries. It seemed a bit cold in décor and stuffy despite all the space. There was also a gloominess to it but that might have been the overcast sky outside and all the snow. The hotel was quite intimidating in size, but I didn't feel scared—I just took it all in.

Later, after check-in, we drove to the Berlin Wall and took photos. Afterward, we drove into East Berlin which had been occupied by Communist Russia. After passing through Checkpoint Charlie, we took in the sights, and immediately I noticed that all the buildings and cars were exactly the same. A scenery of gray, black, and white cars and buildings lined the landscape. It was very dull and empty. If depression were a place, it was East Berlin in 1989. At ten years of age, I understood why people didn't want to live there. I knew tidbits of the history from school and what my parents told me, and that this was a big moment in our lives and in world history. It was hard to grasp all of it as a young kid, without much history under my belt just yet. But the vague, empty grayness of East Berlin could be felt by anyone of any age. Sadness lived there. We drove in silence through the empty streets. It was a ghost town.

During our drive, I saw an amusement park with a sign stating it would open on the same day as my birthday. Maybe one day we'd go back and get on rides. That evening, we ate Chinese food for dinner, which I thought was odd. Whoever thought to go to East Berlin to eat Chinese food? I guess it was the only place around still open.

I loved traveling and seeing new places and still do. Even with its gloominess, the stark, dusty old hotel, deep snow, and empty city, I still had fun. I was with my family, and I don't remember much fighting at all—other than Papi falling asleep with the heater on and having to go to the bathroom outside, I remember feeling lucky to be in a city where history was taking place. Most of all, I remember Papi coming to the back of the van to play with us.

Chapter Five
Song and Dance

When I was sixteen, my Uncle Angel surprised me with a trip to Puerto Rico for my birthday.

"Maritza! Come here!" Mami called from the kitchen. I went over to her and saw that she was on the phone.

"Here, Uncle Angel wants to talk to you," she handed me the phone. Uncle Angel was one of Mami's four brothers. He was the one that made us laugh and made the best Thanksgiving turkeys! I took the phone, excited to talk with him and find out what was going on.

"Hey, Uncle Angel! How are you doing?"

"Hey, Maricita. You wanna go to Puerto Rico?"

"What?! Are you serious?"

"Yes! Happy Birthday!" he said happily.

I screamed and Mami laughed in excitement for me. I was going to Puerto Rico! I couldn't wait. I was so excited to go to the island and see my family. The last time I had been was when I turned a year old and because I didn't have any memory of it, this felt like the first time. Papi let me go so it was all set! I couldn't wait to go and get out of that house!

Mami drove me up to New York and I met up with Uncle Angel and Aunt Candy and her young nephew Dameon who was also going on the trip. I stayed the night at their apartment and the next day we drove to the airport and flew out. I don't remember much about the plane ride, but I do remember liking it. Later, anxiety would take away the enjoyment of flying and replace it with a chilling fear. But at the moment I was enjoying myself. As we began our descent into Puerto Rico, I peered out of the plane window and saw the first palm tree as the island came into view. A sense of calm and belonging came over me at that moment. It was as if a dream was coming true.

Throughout the trip, I had anxiety but I wouldn't know what it was until much later in life. When we arrived at our hotel in San Juan, my grandmother and my aunts (Papi's side of the family) picked me up and took me to a pizza place to eat. I was nervous and had trouble eating all my food. This happened throughout the trip. My stomach felt funny and I began to feel light-headed a lot. I don't remember telling anyone what I was feeling at the time but I now understand the feelings that stirred up my anxiety when I was traveling.

Despite that, the trip was still fun and exciting. Uncle Angel, Aunt Candy, Dameon, and I were invited to our cousin's (on Mami's side of the family) Quinceañera, or "Sweet 15," which was another reason for the trip. A Quinceañera is when a young girl, on her 15th (quince) birthday, becomes a woman in Latin culture and it is celebrated with a big party. Our young cousin, whose birthday it was, got up and sang "No Me Queda Mas (There's Nothing Left for Me)," a song from the late Tejano music star, Selena. Years later, I would sing that same song at my high school talent show.

The place was decorated with butterflies that hung from the ceiling. I cannot remember where it was held but I think it might have been a hall at a hotel along the beach in San Juan. My cousin's dress was pink with lace and her hair was black and in a short smooth shiny bob. She sang the song beautifully and it continues to be one of my favorite songs from Selena. Afterward, we all went out to the dance floor and boogied down! My aunts, Papi's sisters, had taken me days before to the mall and bought me a beautiful white and gray pantsuit with a purse and shoes and fixed my hair in an updo with cascading curls. They did my nails and makeup and bought me a nice lipstick that I had for many years after. They completely spoiled me! Just like Abuelita, they knew how to make my hair beautiful. I guess it's because we all sort of had the same texture of hair. Well! Those curls of mine got stuck in the hanging butterflies and my other cousin, Ray, with whom I was dancing, had to stop dancing and undo my hair from those blasted things! I was so embarrassed, but I kept shaking my hips slightly (We were doing the Merengue) and allowed him to help me. Once I was free, we left the dance floor.

Looking back, it is clear anxiety was with me then, building up over time. Soon, I'd have to learn how to deal with it.

It seemed that worrying was a part of my DNA. Abuelita worried about everything. I guess raising a large family in New York City in the fifties and sixties gave her enough reason for it. She had witnessed a lot of troubles in her life, so I imagine that's why she worried.

Since Abuelita was such a great influence in my life, I learned to think how she thought, which included worrying about what might happen. When my brothers didn't come home by nightfall, I would stay awake with Mami worrying and wondering when they would be home, just like she did as a young girl waiting for her brothers to come home with Abuelita. Not only did we worry whether or not the boys were okay, but we also worried what Papi would do when they came home late. The only reprieve I had from my constant doubt and worry was when I was singing.

Since childhood, I had always dreamed of becoming a professional singer, a pop star. When we lived in El Paso, Janet Jackson was my favorite singer. As I grew up, it changed to Whitney Houston, Selena, Celine Dion, Marc Anthony, and many others. I would try to emulate Selena's musical style. Her music made something come alive in me and I felt like nobody loved her as I did. I wanted to touch people the way she did with music. I wanted people to love my music as they did hers.

Every day in my room after school and on the weekends, I would sing into the radio with her or one of my other favorite singers. Pressing my ear up to the speaker, cherishing the music flowing out like a living river, I would be transformed into a moment in time where I, too, was living my dream. The music spoke to my soul. It was something to hang onto when everything else in life seemed dark and hopeless.

I managed to summon enough confidence to sing in my high school talent shows. Everyone seemed to like me and called me the Selena girl because I would sing only her songs. For one of the shows, I dressed in a white jacket with a red tank top under it and white jeans to sort of mimic her style. The white jacket had a gold zipper and when the best part of the song came on, I unzipped it and revealed my red tank top underneath and danced like Selena to hoots and hollers! It was so much fun. I felt so alive onstage as if that was the only place I truly belonged.

During another show, the CD began skipping. I was singing "Amor Prohibido (Forbidden Love)" when it happened and I looked over at the students who were assisting with the music. They looked at me horrified and mouthed to me they were trying. I wasn't angry, I just told them to stop the CD. Then, the audience began to clap in support but were surprised when I began to finish the song a cappella. Mami was in attendance as she always was cheering me on. At the end of the song instead of singing "Oh Baby," I sang "Oh, Mama," and looked right at her.

The audience erupted in loud applause. I was so proud of myself. It felt so natural to be up there. It felt like there was no other place for me in this world than on stage. It is the place I can express myself. As the curtains open and the sole light shines on me, I tell myself, this is where you belong. It's absolute knowledge and there is no other substitute. All the hurt, pain, depression, and anxiety came out in a beautiful healing way like a small flower that finds a crack in a sidewalk and grows. It finds its place and shines. It's been many years since I have been on stage like that. I wonder if I even know how to do it anymore.

Back then, I put a lot of pressure on myself to sound a certain way. Perfect. I've learned a common trait leading to anxiety and depression is perfectionism. Now, listen, I'm not saying all perfectionists will suffer anxiety and/or depression—that just happened to be a mannerism of mine because of what I went through. When a person is constantly questioning themselves and taking way too long to make simple decisions as I had, it doesn't take long for perfectionism to enter into the game. If I didn't sing smoothly enough, if my voice didn't flow right or I cracked, I'd whip that emotional lash across my heart. After all, this is what I loved to do so I had to do it perfectly! Well, this type of thinking led me to do something very foolish that would lead me to suffer even more—I stopped singing.

The decision happened before I graduated from high school. I was in my room with my sisters and we were living in Washington State. I popped in one of my favorite Celine Dion CDs and pressed play. I began singing with the radio but then she went high and, well, I didn't. I became so frustrated that I could not hit a particular note, I immediately stopped and broke into sobs. My mind spiraled into this negative place where I was talking myself out of my dream. I said "That's it! I'm not doing this anymore!" I had tried for so long to sing well because I believed it was what made me special. I identified singing as my uniqueness.

When I stopped singing, I lost my release, my hope, and my happiness. If I couldn't become a great singer, then what good could I do in this world? Feeling like I had missed my calling, the little confidence I had, began to diminish and my heart broke in two. I ran to the bathroom, slammed and locked the door, and cried myself to sleep on the bathroom floor. Yes, I can be very dramatic, but it was because I did not know how to give myself grace. Control was very important to me, yet I was too inexperienced, young, and ignorant to know how to wield it. This would come with time.

Don't get me wrong, other things made me happy during this time, like my family and friends, but singing was different. When I didn't hit that note, I felt as if God was telling me my dream was dead and to find another. I was crushed. I remember when the dream was first blossoming, telling myself that no one was going to stand in my way but me. Then, I did.

Chapter Six
First Love

Nearing the end of my senior year in high school, I fell in love with my best friend, Javier. We were both from military families and went to the same high school. He was a little taller than me with long black hair, a thin build, and caramel-colored skin. Javier was always happy, laughing and smiling the whole time I knew him in high school. He was and will always be the sweetest most loving person I have ever met.

Although we met in high school, I had considered him as only a friend during that time. He cared for me, but it wasn't until we were both moving away that I realized my true feelings for him ran deeper than friendship. One evening over the phone, he declared his feelings for me.

"I knew right away you were the one for me, the woman I want." His words spilled out easily, matter of factly.

I'm a woman?! Does he see me as a woman?! But we're only graduating high school. Am I a woman? I still feel like a kid.

Reflecting on this conversation years later, I still felt I was a kid, not a grown-up or rather, a woman. I kept wondering who I would be when I was "fully grown up." One day I looked at myself in the mirror and saw the woman that I had become and it shocked me.

I was not shocked because I didn't like what I saw, but because it took me so long to see what was already there. Javier saw her back in school but at twenty-one, I was just starting to notice her. I would later realize the woman looking back at me needed my love. She was no longer the little girl who needed sheltering. She was the woman who needed confidence and assurance, and that could only come from me. My mind took me back to that conversation long ago.

Javier's words hit me and I felt an instant chill of excitement but also fear run through me. What he said was the stuff of romance novels, but I was scared because it meant I had to face what I felt for him. I didn't know what to say. It sounded so easy for him to be vulnerable and proclaim his feelings for me. He was confident enough to tell me exactly how he felt. I, however, wasn't.

"Yes, I know," I replied. *That's it? That's all I had to say? How lame.*

I was frustrated that my feelings were not as concrete, not as simple to proclaim. I somehow knew even then that the day would come when I would see how much I loved him, I just couldn't express it. He saw me as the woman I was becoming, and it scared me.

One afternoon after school, a group of my close friends and I decided to see the movie "Selena." After the movie, my friends and I decided to do something to honor her and our heritage at school. We were in a Latin Heritage group, and we wanted to dedicate a performance to her in which we danced to her music medley from the movie. There were ten of us in the group, but only eight of us performed—four girls and four guys. It was a cultural appreciation assembly performed in front of the entire school in the gymnasium. Each cultural group put together performances to show their heritage through song, dance, and color. We practiced weekly for it.

Javier was my dance partner. We picked out our costumes; the girls wore skirts and cute tops and the guys wore slacks and button-down shirts. My friend and fellow dancer Tricia, who partnered with another friend of mine, Andres, gave me a black flowing shirt that was native to Mexican culture. We did our hair and makeup and I made sure to wear that iconic red lip color Selena always wore. We started the assembly by dancing Salsa to a song by singer Marc Anthony and then finished the performance by dancing to Selena's music.

Javier knew how important Selena was to me, to all of us. I was even allowed to announce our performance when it came time to dance to her music since there was a break between the Salsa and Tejano dancing. During my introduction to the medley part of our performance, I added a little musical rendition of Selena's smash hit, "Bidi Bidi Bom Bom," singing the chorus, which got the crowd hyped up! "Selena, this is for you," I stated before joining my group, forgetting the fears and frustrations I'd felt about singing for a moment.

The energy felt great as I ran back to join the circle my friends made as we did at every practice to start the dance. The girls each had a rose like the one portrayed in the movie. The music started with the medley and the first song was "Como La Flor."

We placed our roses in the center, buds touching. I was feeling so good, not nervous at all—as if performing was just another part of me. As our roses were touching each other, I started to twirl mine around playfully, and then at the right count, we handed our roses to our partners. Then the girls broke off from the guys and turned to face one side of the gymnasium and we danced in tune. When the chorus of the song came, we returned to face the guys, who each handed us our roses, which we then threw back behind them. It was then that I noticed that the rose Javier handed back had lost its bud entirely! When he gave it back to me it was just the stem. I looked at it, made a funny face, and just threw it. The show must go on and it wasn't that big of a deal, but I wished I hadn't twirled it!

The crowd was clapping and cheering, and I fed off of all of that—it gave me more energy and excitement as our performance went on. My confidence was in high gear that day. Then everyone in the gymnasium started singing, "Bidi Bidi Bom Bom" and cheering louder. We finished with Baila Esta Cumbia, dancing to our own choreography perfectly. When we finished and bowed in a straight line, the whole place erupted!

Sometime later we watched the video of our performance at Andres' house, and I saw what went wrong with the rose. When Javier took the rose from me and I turned to dance with the girls, the bud had completely fallen off. We watched as he looked at the other guys and I could see his body language as if he were saying, "Now what do I do? Oh well!" We all laughed at the video. It made for a great memory and a fantastic time. It was during all of those practices that my feelings for Javier grew.

One breezy evening while I was sitting on our deck just outside of the dining room, phone in hand and heart in my throat, I finally declared my feelings for him.

"I wanted to tell you that…I feel the same way as you do. I care about you Javier, very much." I closed my eyes and held my breath waiting for him to respond. He was silent for a few seconds.

"Oh."

"I know, I'm sorry it's taken this long for me to realize it." I suddenly felt defeated.

"No, don't feel bad, it's just that it sucks this happens when we are both moving away. All the time we had in high school we could have been together."

"I know. And I'm sorry, again, it comes at a bad time."

"I understand, sweetheart. You already know how I feel about you."

That was Javier. Always so understanding, patient, and loving. I wished I wasn't so scared about my feelings for him back then.

Chapter Seven
Panic Attack

It was the summer of 1998. I had just graduated from high school and was planning to enter my first year of college in the Fall. Papi had just retired from the U.S. Army. We lived in a split-level house with three bedrooms upstairs, belonging to my brothers and my parents. The large room in the lower portion of the house is where Papi set us girls up. He even put up a partition wall for me so that I had some privacy and built us closets into the walls for our things. Papi was always good with that sort of stuff. We enjoyed our space because it was large and we girls always got along. Ariana's bed was in between mine and Mary's. Anytime I wanted privacy, I could close the plastic brown partition that came between my bed and Ariana's. Some nights when she was scared, I would leave the partition open and hold her hand until she fell asleep.

One morning I was fiercely awakened by my pounding heart and nervousness in my stomach. It felt like I was going to die. The girls had already left for school and I was alone in our room. I was shaking and my mind was racing. I couldn't understand what was happening. I could not control my emotions or thoughts, and an incredible white-hot yet glacial fear overtook me. The nervousness in my stomach felt like hundreds of butterflies moving about inside of me, coupled with the feeling of having my stomach in my throat, like I was on a roller coaster and the ride began its lightning flash descent from the clouds to the ground. I sat up quickly and was in an instant panic. What is this? I was fine last night. Why am I feeling this way? I jumped out of bed due to the adrenaline. I could not stay still. I raced up the stairs as if running from a dark terror or demon, up to my parents' room. As I reached their room, the words bubbled up out of me as I tried to explain to my parents what was going on.

"Mami, I don't feel good. I feel really bad. Can you stay with me today, please?" I desperately pleaded, as if I were still a little kid and wanted to stay with her instead of going to school.

The intensity of the panic attack made me afraid to be alone. Mami consoled me and told me it was going to be okay. She stayed with me. I began to calm down as the day went on. But the next morning, it happened again. This time, Mami couldn't stay with me. This was the first time I felt the dread that would remain with me for many years. I became afraid I would have another panic attack and my first "what if" began that day. I cried as she went down the steps to leave for work.

"What if the feeling comes back?" I asked fearfully.

"Maritza, don't anticipate it. You are going to be okay," she said. Then she gave me her normal blessing with a kiss on the cheek. "I love you and God bless you."

Later that day after the second attack, as I sat in the rocking chair in the living room upstairs, Papi came to give me a hug and began to comfort me. He was very gentle with me as well and told me it was going to be okay. In my fear and many tears, I told him I loved him. Despite the hardships we went through with him, it always bothered him to see us cry and his instinct was to comfort us which he did that very moment as he held me. Mami always told me afterward not to anticipate the attack, but, of course, being told not to think about something only made me likely to think about it even more. It's like saying, "Don't think about the elephant in the room." All I could think about was the elephant!

This anticipation birthed a fear that began to plague me, driving me into numerous panic attacks to the point I never wanted to leave the house. It would take me a long time before I realized not leaving the house was NOT keeping the attacks at bay.

The attacks continued to occur nearly every day for months. I became increasingly aware of them and feared I would have this monster attack me in public, out on the street, or at school. Sometimes they'd begin with my mind feeling fuzzy, then the nausea would come. My "what if" came as if on schedule and was met by a hot/cold feeling that washed over me. I was in a raging river, constantly fighting to keep my head above water.

Sadly, the panic attacks would continue after we left Washington State to start our new lives back east. The fighting between my parents was becoming a daily nuisance and my grandfather, Papi Chi, was having health problems. Papi did not want to move back east but Mami decided not to stay out west any longer. We were leaving Papi again, for the second time in our lives, and driving across the country.

At the time of the move, I had just finished my first year of college and Ezra had graduated from high school. Joshua and Mary were still in high school, and Ariana was in grade school.

When the movers arrived and started packing our stuff, Papi stood at the doorway saddened at what was happening. Mami had told him that we were leaving, but I don't think Papi believed she would go through with it. When he saw the truck, I believe his heart sank.

Of course, we were all excited to leave. It was a chance for us to live a new life without all the fighting. Joshua was laughing at a joke when Mami came into his room to tell us not to look like we were feeling so happy because Papi's heart was breaking. She was crying because even though she was ready to leave he was still her husband and his sadness affected her. Afterwards, we felt bad for not considering his feelings.

I was also saddened when I learned that we would have to leave my beloved dog, Brownie. Dogs weren't allowed in my grandmother's apartment back in New York where we were going. It was breaking my heart to leave him, and I'm sure he knew we were leaving.

"No Brownie, get down. Not today. I know boy, it's okay." As I coaxed his anxious whimpers by stroking his beautiful reddish-brown fur, it was killing me to know I was going to have to get into that van without him. My baby, an Irish Setter. He was so beautiful. Some of the neighbors thought he was female the way he would walk. It was as if he was prancing along with his tail dancing in the air, full of fluff. Thinking about it now brings me to tears. I loved him so much and it hurt me, even more, to think he understood we were leaving.

As we were pulling away, I turned around and looked out the back window at Papi and Brownie. I saw Papi go into the house, but Brownie stayed sitting there at the top of the hill where our house stood. I watched him until he faded from view. Thinking about it now, I realize there were so many sad memories in my young life. We were leaving to find peace and happiness, but my heart was torn, and a part of me was left behind that day. My dog just sat there and watched us leave. When I wonder if he thought he did something wrong, my heart breaks all over again.

Mami's bravery once again amazed me. She and my brother, Ezra, drove us all from Seattle, Washington to New York City.

Chapter Eight
Far From Full

I didn't have my driver's license at the time, I was a late bloomer. During the ride, I kept thinking that once we got back to the East Coast, I would be better. I had to be better.

But throughout the whole trip, I was not able to finish my meals and was constantly nervous. Half-eaten plate after half-eaten plate was thrown away because of my nervousness. Mami mentioned that it was getting expensive to throw away so much food, but I couldn't help it. I was constantly nauseated. I felt guilty for not being able to finish my food, ashamed that I was throwing it away and I argued with myself. *Please just eat one more bite! This is so exhausting. I just can't. I don't know what to do. Is this my life now? Each day we get closer to New York, to our new lives but I just can't seem to leave this behind!* I felt defeated every day and wondered what was on the other side of the country for me.

I tried to divert my thoughts to attending the university I was transferring to as a sophomore, Towson State University in Maryland. But thinking about school was part of the problem. The thought of living on campus away from my siblings and Mami scared me. I didn't want to be without her, especially when I relied upon her strength to get through the day. I didn't believe I was strong enough.

As the journey continued, I'd lose myself in the scenery. Idaho and Montana were beautiful, but Montana is a very long state to drive through. I thought we would never get across it. The greenery and the mountains were captivating. Then, North Dakota... grass and sky. As we started to see the eastern portion of the country, the drive seemed to go by faster. We drove through Minnesota where I read the license plates stating it was the land of ten thousand lakes. *Yeah, whatever dude, I only counted twenty on this route!* In Wisconsin, I had such a yearning for cheese, but my meal didn't come with any at our lunch stop. I begged Ezra for a bit of the cheese off of his steak. Of course, he said no.

With each state we passed through I would collect a key chain as a souvenir. Soon, we passed through Chicago where we hit our first traffic jam at a toll booth plaza. Man, there was no traffic until we got here. Then, into Indiana, Ohio, and Pennsylvania, another long state to drive across. By God's grace, we made it to my grandparents' apartment in the Bronx, New York. Boy, were we glad for that ride to be over! Could you imagine? Driving in a luggage-packed van with six people on limited funds and no GPS? We roughed it using a USA Road Maps book. We could have broken down or run out of money just like we did when we left El Paso many years ago, only making it to Arkansas. God was surely with us. This time, Mami didn't turn around. This time, we made it to New York.

Mami knew she didn't want to stay in New York City though, so she secured us a residence in Aberdeen, Maryland where we lived previously before heading out to Seattle. She transferred her job as a customer service employee with the Internal Revenue Service from the Seattle office to the Baltimore office, and soon, Ezra got a job at the mess hall at Aberdeen Proving Ground. I, too, secured employment at the local Target. I wanted to work there because walking into it made me think of Washington State. Every Target is built the same so when I entered the store, I would pretend I was still in the Pacific Northwest. Even after everything that happened, I missed the beauty of that place.

Joshua, Mary, and Ariana were enrolled in school and soon life back east fell into a comfortable routine. But not for me. I didn't like being back in Aberdeen because it felt like going back in time, where I didn't want to be. Yet, at least life was more peaceful this time around without Papi.

We'd call him periodically to see how he was doing and sometimes, he would even put the phone to Brownie's ear so that I could talk to him. When Brownie heard his name through the phone, he barked excitedly. It made me miss him more.

My initial hope that the attacks would go away when we relocated to the east coast died quickly and new anxieties arrived daily. Now in Maryland, I realized I was severely depressed and in a constant state of anxiety.

The house we rented became my only comfort zone. If I was home, there was nothing I couldn't handle. At home, I felt nothing could hurt me. But out of my fear of leaving the house, I stopped doing the things I loved to do like go to the movies or even go out with my friends; depression was taking over my life.

I knew the reality deep down, that I'd trapped myself in the house. Everyone else left daily to work or school and life continued for them. I often cried out of desperation and hopelessness. I realized that the constant crying was not natural or healthy. Also, my appetite was again leaving me and I started to lose weight. Since I was already so thin, I feared I would never eat again and die of thinness. In my mind, I equated skinniness with death because I thought I was wasting away. This was one more thing for me to fear. I didn't want to die.

In turn, the crying, the not eating, and the growing fear of looming death caused many more panic attacks. Every time I couldn't eat because of my nerves, I would panic because I didn't want to lose any more weight. One day, all I had were two crackers to eat and a few sips of water to drink. I knew this would not be good for me in the long run, but my nerves prevented me from being able to eat or drink much more. I somehow convinced myself those two crackers were enough and I was ok.

I also hated being skinny. When I was younger, people would say what a blessing it was to be thin, but all I could associate thinness with was the fear I harbored of wasting away. It got to the point that I began to fear I was becoming anorexic. I understood anorexia was a disease often stemming from a person's fear of being overweight, but the irony was, I wanted to be overweight! Why did I think I was anorexic? As I reflect on those times, I realize anorexia was a label I needed to put on something that I did not understand.

My lack of understanding of my condition led me to wonder, why does everyone else have it all together? *What's wrong with me? Nobody goes through what I am going through.* Or so I thought.

Mami became very worried about me and would tell me how much she loved me all the time. I knew my anxiety and depression were hurting her, too. She saw her bright, beautiful daughter, full of life, quickly being reduced to a closed, dull shell. I felt like I couldn't do anything about it, but Mami was always strong. Oh, how I wished I could be strong like her. She was able to use laughter to get through the hard times. She was always joking and getting along with everyone, but it was hard for her to laugh when she saw me depressed. She cried because she felt helpless. I, in turn, would feel even worse because I was making her upset.

I couldn't get my head above water. Not knowing how to tread water, I was drowning in my own misery.

In her ongoing effort to help me through the struggle, Mami gave me an 800 toll-free phone number she saw on a commercial about depression. At my wit's end and willing to do anything to survive the depression, I decided to call. I spoke to a nice lady who referred me to my first psychiatrist and therapist. I made my first appointment and was later prescribed Paxil. Paxil is an antidepressant that would help me for many years to come.

My therapist was a very nice, tall lady with shoulder-length dusty brown hair and friendly eyes. Her face was round and she had a soft appearance. I could see her compassion as I began explaining my struggle with the constant sadness and fears. I felt much better afterward letting everything out. I instantly liked her and felt heard.

"What is a normal day like for you? Tell me what emotions you feel."

"Well, I wake up with nausea caused by being nervous. I don't even know why I am nervous. I can't eat and don't eat for most of the day because I'm nauseous. Then I get scared because if I don't eat, I think I'll die. And it snowballs from there."

"Why don't you concentrate on one thing at a time and not jump into the future? Your hunger will come. I want you to start to believe that" she said softly.

"Okay," I responded. It sounded impossible but what else did I have to lose?

As time went on, things seemed to improve for me. I was less anxious being on the medication. However, the fear of panic attacks still loomed, so, at the request of my therapist, I bought a book by Dr. Claire Weekes entitled *Hope and Help for Your Nerves*. To be truthful, the book didn't help me much at first. It wasn't until many years later when I had learned more about my condition, I came back to the book and was able to understand what the author was saying.

My sessions with my therapist, the medication, and my research led me to see that my condition affected many other people as well. Finally, I was starting to learn that I was not the only one. It felt good knowing I was not alone. During this time, I didn't move onto the college campus at Towson. In fact, I needed more credits to be able to transfer as a sophomore, so I enrolled at Harford Community College. I went to school part-time there while working at Target. I began to fall into a routine and for the first time, feel normal again.

My bosses were so pleased with my work that they promoted me. I was excited at first about the promotion, but soon grew fearful of messing up or disappointing my boss, and the panic attacks returned.

One day I was called in to work as a cashier. I normally worked out on the floor but the cashier supervisor needed help so I told her I would come in for four hours to help. After I had signed on to the cash register, I remember looking down at my tummy. I wore a red fitted blouse and noticed, or thought, my tummy looked sunken in. Of course, this was all in my head. Again, I began to equate my thinness with being sick and dying.

As that thought registered in my brain the familiar body symptoms of the panic attack started; the nervousness and nausea, the pounding heart, and sweaty palms. I became very nervous, and I told the supervisor I was not feeling well, hoping she would let me go home. I was the only cashier on duty at the time so she told me she couldn't. I felt foolish even asking her if I could leave after telling her previously, I would help out. That foolish feeling added guilt to the panicky feelings.

My first customer came into my line and started putting her items onto the belt. I felt the adrenalin rush through my body and my face flushed hot. I knew I had to perform my duties now and there was no way to get out of it. I thought I would pass out from the effects of the mounting attack. The adrenalin awakened my senses to a total alert level. It was as if the "code red" alarm was sounding off inside me. My mind raced with the duties I had to perform and with trying to control what I was feeling so that the customer would not notice. This took more energy than the attack itself. The fear intensified and I wanted to cry out in frustration. My palms were sweaty and my hands began to shake as I picked up each item and brought it across the scanner. *Why does she have to have so much stuff?* I thought to myself. *I can't do this right now! Oh, God! Please help me through this! Will it ever end?*

It did end, finally. I stayed and finished out my four hours and went home feeling a bit better but exhausted.

But the depression returned due to my lack of confidence in myself, and I began missing a lot of work. I explained to my boss what was going on in my life, and she was sympathetic, but she had a boss of her own to answer to and a store to run. I felt like my job was on the line.

I began to worry about my job. It made my nervousness even worse and, once again, I started losing my appetite. As a result of not eating, I would feel lightheaded, lose focus on the job and at school, and lose my desire to go to work. I missed days at work here and there due to the physical symptoms. I didn't want to lose my job and I was afraid one day I would.

> *Journal Entry: 1/18/00*
> *I didn't go to work today because again, I feel terrible.*
> *I don't know why I worry or let my nerves control me. If*
> *this keeps up, I won't have a job much longer.*

Looking back now, I felt alone in my condition, and I didn't know how to get out of it. I had my family, and they loved me, but they didn't understand what was going on with me.

Eventually, I asked to be demoted to a position with less responsibility. I believed that decreasing the stress from work would help reduce my anxiety and depression. Unfortunately, the depression intensified. Instead of feeling less stressed, I began to feel guilty for not being able to perform in a higher position. I had let myself down and let my employer down, too. I could feel myself going downhill. How could I be doing so well to be promoted, only to lose it all to fear?

Not being able to eat much, I was losing weight again. At 20 years old I now weighed just ninety-eight pounds, my high school weight. I got on the scale every morning praying I would gain a pound despite the fact I hadn't eaten any more yesterday than the day before.

My life was not my own. One day, I was three hours late for work because I was waiting on a taxicab. I couldn't call out because I had already talked with my boss about my frequent absences. I was at home feeling lightheaded and was trying to force myself to eat. I removed a frozen dinner out of the freezer and stuck it in the microwave. *This should be easy to get down.* I sat at the table looking down at the meal feeling defeated. *Okay Maritza, just eat as much as you can. It's okay. God, how am I going to swallow this food with this knot in my throat? Just thinking about it makes me want to puke!* I began eating finally and hoped for the vaguely familiar feeling of a full tummy, but it never came. Okay, I ate it but why am I still lightheaded? Moody and irritable, I then realized I had run out of Paxil and was feeling the side effects. The cab never came to take me to work.

Mami ended up coming home from the store to take me in. When I arrived at work, the store manager took me to the side and had another talk with me. He reminded me once more about the previous talk I had with my supervisor, yet he was still very kind and understanding.

"Maritza, you're three hours late. Remember we talked about your tardiness and absences. I believe you can do better." He said gently.

"I know, John," I replied in a small voice as I looked down at the floor feeling like a waste of space, a disappointment. "I'm trying, I'll do better. I'm so sorry."

He tried to lighten the conversation by bringing up my goal of buying my first car. "How's the car search going? I know you will find the right one. Soon you'll be driving here on your own and it will be great!" He was more enthusiastic about it than I was at that moment. He was very kind yet despite him trying to force life into my future, the defeat I felt was so heavy, his positive words could not penetrate the fortress of darkness that surrounded me.

Looking back on that now, I see that God was with me then. How many managers would keep being kind to someone who kept messing up? I didn't mean to mess up, I just could not escape the hell in which I felt trapped.

After the talk with John, I felt worthless because I thought I had disappointed him again. Although he was positive, all I could think about were my failures. When I went to my assigned section that day, I began thinking of ending it all when I got home that evening. Incredibly unhappy with myself, my work, and feeling that I'd let everyone down, I convinced myself I would not be alive the next day.

I allowed the thought of taking my life to enter my mind. It came gently without pushing and I let down the drawbridge to the fortress in which I was trapped and welcomed it like a comforting friend. I did not know how the end would come but believed it would happen, nonetheless. I wasn't afraid of ending my life, but a blanket of sadness covered me. As I worked in the aisles, straightening the products slowly, the thought of a bottle of pills came to mind: *Maybe I could take some pills. I want something that won't hurt. I want to fall...drift away easily. Then lie down and sleep.... forever.*

I realize now that the sadness I felt was due to the fact I still loved myself. Even if my love was just a little, it was still a flicker of hope in my otherwise hopeless life.

Chapter Nine
Butterfly Kisses

Time seemed to slow down and become fuzzy for me. While wandering in a haze of gloom, something significant happened that same day while at work. A gentleman looking for a Panasonic phone approached me. I was not in the mood to be cheerful and give the best customer service, but he was very nice to me so I felt I could deal with him at least. When I went to check to see if we had the phone, I noticed a gray dot on the price tag on the shelf. Gray dots meant the product was not in stock and there was a good possibility it was not coming back.

As I walked him to the Guest Services counter to help him fill out a rain check for the item, I explained to him he would be called if the item was restocked. He began to chit-chat with me about other various things. He was an older gentleman with white hair and glasses. I felt a very easy vibe coming from him as if I was safe with him. As our general conversation continued, it took a turn:

"Are you Hispanic?" he asked gently with a welcoming smile.

"Yes, I am," I replied, curious about the question.

"Do you know of the picture of the Virgin Mary? The one with the roses surrounding her?"

I knew about the picture. It is the picture of La Virgin de Guadalupe or The Virgin of Guadalupe. The story of the picture is that she appeared to a man in Mexico centuries ago near a rose bush. I wondered where he was going with all of this.

"Yes, I know of that picture," I responded.

"Do you know that you are one of those roses?" he asked.

I was silenced by his words and for a moment, time stood still. I didn't know what to say to that. He seemed so happy just being around me. Who says things like this?

It's not every day a person gets told by a kind stranger she is a rose belonging around the Virgin Mary! I instantly knew then God had intervened. Who else could spiritually grab me like that? God knew the intentions in my heart—thoughts of suicide—and He stopped it from happening. Why? Because He loves me and my story was not over. It was only beginning. He knew that I would write this memoir with the desire to help others struggling like I was. My purpose on Earth was not complete. I later learned from my supervisor the same gentleman left a kind compliment on my service with the front desk. What's amazing is that I didn't even feel like I did my best! God knows where we are every moment—in mind, body, and spirit. When He sees us in trouble, He sends down His angels to remind us of His love. His love rescued me.

That afternoon after work, I told Mami about it on our way to Taco Bell—my appetite was back! I started to feel better and became chatty in the van on the ride home. Mami encouraged me, saying God always shows up when we need Him. I didn't tell her about my suicidal thoughts though. After that encounter, my spirit lifted and the thought of taking my life left exactly the way it came—across the drawbridge. A little bit of sunlight pierced through the clouds to shine on my fortress, moving darkness aside for the time being. I call this a "butterfly kiss from God" because it was light and beautiful, bringing back the color before my eyes like a butterfly's wings.

As fall arrived and I continued my college courses at Harford Community College, I unexpectedly met someone in one of my classes. His name is Mark. We were both taking a geography class. He was a tall, dark, and handsome fellow who was nine years my senior.

One night after class, while I waited for Ezra to pick me up to go home, Mark came over and spoke to me for the first time. Ezra must have forgotten about me because I was standing outside for quite a while when Mark asked me if I needed a ride. At first, I said no because I didn't know him, but as we began to talk more, I instantly felt at ease with him. I learned that he was a soldier in the Army and played music. He also told me he had been contemplating asking me out, but he had been too nervous to do it. Smiling at this, I wondered if he was going to ask me out at that moment. I gave him my number so that we could help each other in class. Help each other in class? Uh, yeah right! Can we say move along anxiety; Maritza is finally going to start dating?

As the night began to get chilly and the lights to the classroom buildings went out, it was apparent Ezra was not coming. I reluctantly decided to allow Mark to take me home. Mark was very respectful and acted appropriately with me. I felt very comfortable with him as he drove me home. I found myself smiling a lot as we talked. When I got home, I made myself something to eat (oatmeal because it was easy to make and filling) because suddenly, I wanted to take better care of myself so I could discover this new thing happening with Mark.

I had never really dated anyone other than the long-distance relationship I had experienced with my high school love, Javier. It wasn't long before Mark called to ask me out. I remember I was talking to my sister about him when the phone rang, and it was him! We talked for a while, and then he asked me to go to the movies with him. Of course, I said yes.

Excited to go on my first real date, I told Mami about him and that he was coming to pick me up. Well, Mami wanted to meet him, and I thought, ugh, this is only the first date, and I'm twenty! He's gonna think I'm nuts! But Mark was nice about it, and I asked him to come inside. He and Mami said hello and she liked him instantly. After my date, she would go on to tell me that she immediately got on the phone with Abuelita because she had to tell her all about it! Mark and I began dating, going to movies and dinners, and I was starting to feel happy and at ease for the first time in a long while. I had something else to busy my mind with other than the depression.

I held out on kissing him for a while because I didn't want to move too fast. He said he liked that about me. He told me one of the things he liked most about me was my virtue. Our first kiss finally happened at the movies one afternoon. It was my first real kiss, and I was nervous because I wasn't sure if I knew what I was doing.

"Are you feeling, okay?" he whispered. "The movie is almost over." He knew I was getting nervous again.

"Yes, I'm okay," I replied quietly as my heart began to beat fast, the panic symptoms starting. They began with the lone thought that I had not eaten much that day. Earlier in the day, I'd eaten tomato soup and some bread. I was afraid I would pass out in front of him. How embarrassing! That was all it took for the anxiety to kick in.

He knew what I was going through because I had shared a little of my battles openly with him. He was very understanding and easy to talk to, and I needed someone to confide in other than my family. The movie theater was large and there were only a few people there aside from us. We didn't get any popcorn because I wasn't sure I was going to be able to eat it. He put his arm around me gently. I looked over at him, and slowly, he leaned into me until our faces were only a breath apart. Then he kissed me ever so gently and fully. It was like slow motion. I was so enthralled with the kiss, my mind far from any feelings of guilt or fear. They were replaced with feelings of want and desire. I liked those feelings much more.

The relationship would last but a few short blissful months. Mark was soon stationed overseas, and we had to say our goodbyes. But I realized that throughout our brief courting, I began to feel better about life in general and began to feel more like a woman. I still had problems with my nerves, but I was feeling happier, and more optimistic. Mami took notice of the change in me and knowing that I was happy made her happy, too.

Mark and I remained very good friends, and I enjoyed the times we had together because he made me want more of those good feelings. I will always remember him fondly. I was blessed to have him in my life during a time of struggle. I knew he was yet another butterfly kiss from God and I would need many of those to get through what was coming next.

Chapter Ten
Not a Friend of Planes

After Mark left, I wanted to travel and visit Javier, who had remained my friend all this time. Yet my anxiety and depression kept me from doing so. There were times when fear interfered with my desire to travel.

I was scheduled to visit Javier in Texas not long after the events of 9/11 occurred. But regardless of my desire to see him, I couldn't get on the plane. I told him that it was because of the events of 9/11, which was partially true. Because of anxiety, I grew increasingly fearful of airplane rides, imagining them ending in a horrible crash. I was also afraid of having panic attacks while in flight and being away from home. My head was filled with so many "what if" scenarios, that I allowed fear to overtake my desire to see Javier.

At the airport, I had made it to the security line where Mami could no longer travel with me. I looked back at her, fear in my eyes, love, and compassion in hers. The security lady told me to move up and I just couldn't.

"I, uh, I'm sorry, I can't," I stammered, and crying, went back to Mami. The security lady was understanding and let me go back.

"What do you want to do Flaca?" Mami asked softly. "Flaca" is another nickname for me that Mami and Papi used. It means skinny girl but is always said as an endearment, full of love.

"I want to go home with you," I replied through my tears.

"Okay, it's okay. Let's go," she said. That's Mami. So easy and loving. She didn't push or make me feel bad. It was whatever I wanted and needed when I struggled. At that moment, I needed her and her strength. *I'll figure it all out when we get home. I know I have to call him. I just want to get home.*

When Mami and I got back home from the airport, I knew what I had to do. *There's no use in prolonging it. I need to tell him before he goes to the airport.* Feeling awful and fearful, I dialed Javier's number. I waited for the phone to ring. Not going to see him was one of the hardest things I ever had to do because we were both looking forward to it. As the phone rang, my heart began beating fast. What would I say?

"Hey! My sister is helping me get everything ready for you here at the house," he said excitedly.

"Hi, Javier. I have something to tell you. I...I am not gonna make it. I'm...I'm so sorry." The words stumbled out of my mouth. He was silent. Suddenly negative thoughts filled my head. *Gosh, you really know how to mess things up, don't you? How are you gonna tell him on the day that you are supposed to leave that you are not going? He is waiting for you! What's the matter with you?*

I hated myself. I needed a good excuse. Being nervous and depressed with anxiety was not a good excuse—at least, not to me at the time. I didn't know how to share this part of me with him yet. I needed to switch it off, but I couldn't.

"It's just...I got scared in the security line. I jumped out. Thinking about what happened in September just really got to me. I'm sorry. I'm so sorry, Javier," I said with a broken heart.

I felt guilty for laying this on him and for my feelings of insecurity and fear. I didn't want to lose control of my emotions while on the plane or while visiting him, and I knew I did lose control when I had panic attacks. I imagined the onslaught of emotions I'd feel if a panic attack occurred and did whatever I could to avoid the storm. As I was speaking with him, I could feel the depression looming above me, slowly descending like a dark cloud. I then felt it in my head, right over my brow. A heaviness I couldn't escape. I was letting him down—the person I loved.

"Oh, okay," he said, half confused, half disappointed.

The heaviness overtook me and I ended the call quickly. *I have to lie down. I have to sleep.* The weight of it all made my body sink into the bed. *This is where I belong now. Close your eyes and drift away. Escape. Don't worry about tomorrow or Javier. It's okay. Sleep. No more worries.*

But sleep never lasted. I woke up and had to deal with the sadness and the self-questioning all over again. Most of all, I had to deal with the many emotions waiting to be felt.

Sometime after, Mami went back west to visit Papi and talk about their relationship. They were still married but we were living on opposite sides of the country. Mami needed help at home financially and support from Papi. They both still loved each other. After her visit, he decided to sell the house and drive back east with her. They were going to give their marriage another shot.

I felt anxious about Papi coming back into our lives. We had peace at home without his anger. When we came back to Maryland after leaving Papi, Mami found a nice, simple yet large white house with three bedrooms, a sunroom, a large attic, and a basement for us to live in. Mary and Ariana shared one room. I had one and Mami had hers. The boys stayed up in the attic. The rent for the place was only $700. I never really told her at the time how proud I was of her. We only had one van and Ezra would take it for work while Mami would walk down to the train station and take the MARC train into Baltimore to her job. She always made it work out. As time went by, the expenses of living in Maryland were catching up to us. Even with three of us kids working, me, Ezra, and Joshua, Mami still needed help. Papi was still paying a mortgage on our house in Washington, and it seemed to be a waste of money. So, she began talking about the possibility of Papi coming to live with us again.

"But what if he starts up his fighting again?" I asked. "You know how he can be."

"Maritza, it's hard out here. Maryland is very expensive, and I was not going to move you guys to the Bronx. I'm going to Washington to have a talk with your father and figure out what he wants to do. Now that he sees I wasn't playing around by leaving him, maybe he will be better this time." she said.

I knew she still loved him and he loved her, but I also knew he hadn't changed.

"Okay," I said. I decided to pray about it.

The time came and she flew out to Washington. I guess the talk went well because before we five kids knew what was going on, they packed up his belongings, grabbed the dog, hitched up his old Mercedes to a moving truck, and the three of them drove to Maryland. I was excited to see Brownie, yet not sure how I felt about Papi coming back into our lives. The day arrived and I saw the moving truck pull up in front of our white house with his car attached to it. I opened the door excitedly as my beautiful boy,

Brownie, danced in like he already lived there. I began to hug him and noticed how fat he was! Joshua came downstairs and began to pet Brownie, welcoming him too. As Brownie realized who Joshua was, he began to cry in excitement. I was so happy to see my dog again and had missed him so much. Mami and Papi came in and all of us were together again.

After the drive and things settled down, Papi lay on the couch to relax after the long trip. Wanting to talk to him and not knowing the right thing to say, I knelt at his side and asked, "Are you gonna be good this time?" I was worried that he would start the fighting up again.

"What do you mean, good this time? I'm not a child," he said sarcastically. Then he drifted off to sleep. I realized then and there that nothing had changed. The fights continued throughout the years as they had in the past.

After Papi came to live with us again, Javier and I decided to have another go at our relationship and he came to visit me.

"I miss seeing you. When do you think we can see each other again?" I asked over the phone.

"Well, I could come to visit you. I just need to be invited," he said with amusement.

How could I not realize that I hadn't invited him? He had always invited me to Texas and for some reason, I couldn't understand why the idea of inviting him did not occur to me.

"Oh! Of course, you're invited! Will you come?" I asked excitedly.

"Yes, sweetheart! I'll start looking at tickets!"

I told my parents that my 'friend' was coming to visit. With Papi back in the house, I didn't want to say 'boyfriend' because he was too strict when it came to his girls dating and I didn't want to deal with it. Papi did his best to make up a spare room with a bed in the sunroom for Javier. I was surprised at how hospitable he was, and I appreciated it.

The day came and I was so nervous I couldn't even drive my newly purchased car to get Javier so Mami, always there for me, drove me to pick him up at the airport. As soon we drove up to the curb and I saw him standing there my heart beat so fast, and the adrenaline that usually coursed through me during a panic attack appeared as excitement instead. I waved my arm out of the window at him like a crazy person and he happily waved back! We stopped and I embraced him tightly for all the moments lost to us in the past, the days we missed each other and every moment yet to come. I was incredibly happy to see him again. We finally got in my car and Mami drove us back to the house.

Javier and I had a wonderful time together. We would go on walks and drive around my town. We went out for dinners and just enjoyed being in each other's presence. I introduced him to Miriam who was one of my best friends. I met her while working at Target. I worked on the sales floor and she was a cashier. She is bubbly yet fierce at times. Miriam liked Javier. She told me she could see how much we loved each other, and it made her very happy to see me happy.

Finally, it was our last night together. We were on the way home from dinner riding in the back of our family van. Javier and I just sat and held each other, and I closed my eyes savoring the moment. In that moment my heart burst with love for him. The next day he would be on a flight back home to Texas.

We embraced each other and said our goodbyes in the early morning hours before the sun rose, and then he was gone.

Chapter Eleven
Loved and Lost

After he left, we tried to date long distance again. It was hard at times because the space between us made our future together unclear. I imagine that he, too, was frustrated with me because he would often ask me where things stood between us.

I knew deep down inside that I loved him dearly. Javier and I had been through a lot together, and we were great friends and we had history. When I would go to visit him in Texas, (yes, when I finally did get on the plane!) I knew that he was my man and that a future with him was what I wanted. Once I returned home though, my feelings about our future became less clear. Dealing with anxiety and self-esteem issues, it was hard for me to make decisions and my mind would feel foggy.

Feeling confused and angry at myself, I sought advice from my friend Miriam.

"Maritza, the only way you two are going to work out is if you pack up and move down there to Texas to be with him," she said.

I thought about her words and was silent. I believed it was true. But I didn't believe I could do it. After all, it was a daily struggle dealing with my own mind. I was afraid the panic attacks would get worse if I did move and I didn't have the confidence to deal with them so far away from Mami. I was afraid to be away from my family. Mami and my brothers and sisters were my support system.

When he visited me, it was like I was on a constant "high," but when he left, I felt empty. He was the key, the trigger, the main ingredient to my happiness at the time. But without him, it was harder to maintain that feeling.

Often, I wished I hadn't confused or frustrated him about where we stood. He was always so kind, gentle, and patient with me, and he had always loved me for who I was. While having a conversation on the phone one day, he expressed to me his frustration, yet as always, he did it gently.

"I get mixed signals from you. I never know where I stand with you," he said, concerned.

"I know and I am sorry. I just know that when I am with you, I know exactly what I want—it's you. But when we're apart it just seems so complicated for me," I confessed.

As time continued, I eventually transferred from Harford Community College to Towson University to complete my studies for my bachelor's degree in Geology. One day, while on campus, I ran into someone from my past. Darren was a member of the same church in Maryland I attended as a child, and we were in the same CCD Sunday school class before I moved out west with my family. I hadn't seen him in years and now, he reappeared in my life. He was tall and blonde with an infectious smile. Darren was very sweet, an awesome cook, and he was quite funny. We started to become reacquainted, this time as young adults and our feelings for each other began to move beyond friendship. I wanted to date him, but I didn't want to be disloyal to Javier. So, one day I called Javier and told him about Darren.

"So, I met someone at school. I want to experience dating. I just hate that we can't date the way we want. I don't know what to do but I knew I had to tell you." I was close to tears. This was harder than I thought it would be. But again, Javier, ever patient and kind, was understanding. His response flung open the floodgates.

"I understand, sweetheart. I can't expect to keep you forever." I could hear the tears in his voice. "Go ahead and date him. It's okay, baby."

In tears and unable to hide my emotion, I just sobbed on the phone. All I could think about was not hurting him and how I hated the whole situation. When I hung up, I just sat on my bed at home and continued to cry. I could feel my heart breaking. I wanted to date Darren because he was here, but I still loved Javier.

Why couldn't we live in the same state so we could be together? If we did, our hearts wouldn't be breaking. Am I being selfish? Do high school sweethearts really last? I felt guilty that I didn't try harder to make the relationship work. But what if I didn't date Darren, and Javier and I stayed together? How long would it be before he met someone in Texas, and he would be the one calling me?

Javier and I ended our dating relationship again…for the fourth or fifth time, I don't know, I had lost count…but we remained friends.

Darren and I began to date and soon I began to care for him very much. We had great times in Towson—going from school to work to hanging out together at the movies, making dinners, and spending time with mutual friends. At one of my girlfriend's birthday parties, Darren got up and sang karaoke while I cheered him on. I needed that at the time. It was nice having someone to share times with and talk to. But our relationship wouldn't last beyond a year or so. Although we cared for each other, our lives were going in different directions once he left school.

Towards the end of my relationship with Darren, Javier told me that he had met someone and was dating. I couldn't be upset because I was doing the same thing. We still called each other occasionally to see how the other was doing. Not long after Darren and I had broken up, I learned that Javier was getting married.

I found out when our mutual friend Andres, whom we had traveled a few years earlier to see graduate in El Paso, called to give me the news.

"Hey Flacabella," he said. Flacabella or "beautiful skinny girl" was what my friends from the Latin Heritage Group in high school called me. Sometimes my friends would shorten it to Flaca. We had nicknames for everyone and Andres was Guero Loco or just Guero.

"Hey, Guero! How are you doing?"

"Good." He sounded a little serious and concerned.

"What's wrong? Everything okay?" I could feel he had something to tell me, but I couldn't tell what.

"Yeah, I'm okay. I just have some news. Javier is getting married, and they want to start a family."

"Oh," I replied. What can you say to that? I was silent for a minute. Andres and I continued to chat a little longer before we got off the phone. I sat on my bed almost in the same position as I did when I told Javier I wanted to date Darren. I looked at the wall. I was crestfallen. Then the thoughts started. *It's all your fault. You couldn't hold on to him. He is so good! You lost him!* I didn't know what to think or say so once again, I just let the tears fall.

A few weeks later at work, Javier called. I saw his number on my cell and my heart stopped. I didn't expect him to call. I could only imagine what he was going to say. I excused myself from my workstation and went outside so I could talk to him in private.

"Hey. How are you doing? I know you know about Melissa and me, but I wanted to call you and talk to you myself."

"Hi. I'm doing okay. Yes, I know."

"Remember when we said that if we didn't marry each other we would go to each other's weddings as friends?"

We did say that, but we were kids in high school not realizing it probably wouldn't be a good idea. But then again, we were best friends first and always supported one another.

"Yes, I do," I said, knowing where this was going. I sucked in my breath for his invitation.

"I would like you to come," he said gently.

One beat, two beats, three…. breathe, Maritza.

"Javier…. thank you for the invite but…. I'm not sure I can go. I can't take off work and school and I don't have the money right now for the plane ticket. I'm sorry. Congratulations on your wedding," I said sadly.

Of course, I lied. I could go but knew that wouldn't be the best thing for me to do mentally or emotionally.

"Oh okay," he replied, a hint of sadness in his voice.

We chatted a few more minutes before he said something I would remember for many years:

"I guess we're not meant to be." It was matter of fact. Final.

"I guess we're not," I said, my heart breaking again at the realization that this was really the end and I had finally lost him for good.

We ended the conversation wishing each other well. For many months afterwards, I wondered what life would have been like if I had never let him go — if I became his wife. I thought about it a lot.

While I grieved the loss of what could have been, I finally came to a place of acceptance because at the end of the day I had to. I could not blame him for life taking over. He was happy and that was important to me.

Because of God's presence in my life, I had the strength to move on after I realized I had lost Javier forever. I was beginning to see that life wasn't always what I wanted it to be and that I had to live with my choices. I guess I was growing up.

I decided to be single for a while and focus on my studies. I would need all the focus possible to finish college. I struggled with the constant thought that I would never graduate. My grades were low in my core classes and I had to take a few courses multiple times. As my classmates began graduating one by one and I was still at school, I started to think maybe I just wasn't smart enough. Graduation seemed so far away. Am I going to make it, or am I just fooling myself?

Chapter Twelve
Good Cop, Bad Cop

One afternoon, I was in my parents' room, lying in bed watching
TV with my younger sister, Ariana. Mary had left to clean out her
car and my brothers were out as well. Mami was at work. It was
just Ariana and me. Then Papi came into the room in a foul mood.
He was angry because he couldn't find Mary. He started yelling,
bad-mouthing the world, and throwing things:

Journal Entry: 10:51, 8/22/2004
Papi starts getting upset because Mary is gone. As
always, he starts yelling at me because of it. I'm angry
at Mary for being away from the house because he's
taking it out on me. He yells at me because I don't always
know where she is. He keeps going on and on about how
horrible his life is and how ungrateful we all are. He just
won't shut up! I keep holding my tongue and holding
back until finally I just can't anymore and I BLOW UP.
"Then kill me, kill me if your life is so miserable!" I yell.
Ariana cowers in a corner crying and holding her hands
up to her ears. I want to be put out of my misery. But then
he rushes towards me, grabs me around my shoulders,
shakes me hard a few times, and silences me with a single
burning slap across my face. Papi never hit me in the face

before. I am stunned. "You're a college girl, you should be smart enough not to take this so personally. You are out of control!" Me, out of control? Imagine that. After he leaves, I go to the mirror to check out the damage. A perfect hand outline marks my cheek. "You see this, Ariana? This is how all our spankings were--hand marks on our legs and bottoms." I just never thought I'd see one again.

He told me that he hit me because I was getting too emotional, that I was losing control, but I knew he wanted the confrontation to justify his anger. At that moment, I hated him and glared at him hoping he could see how much I did. I regretted it later. No matter how bad it was, I could never really hate Papi. I didn't tell Mami for some time. I didn't want it to create more stress and problems between them because there was enough of that for one day. But there would be more of those days to come, more fighting.

One evening as I walked in the front door coming home from my college classes, Joshua and Papi were having a heated discussion. I arrived in the middle of their conversation. Later, Joshua told me it started with him voicing his opinion, which was contrary to that of Papi's.

"You don't know what you're talking about! You are just spoiled!" Papi shouted. I sat on the armrest of the couch. I positioned myself at the edge of the living room in full view of what was going on, ready to jump in if needed to protect my brother. Fear crept up inside me and my right knee started to shake as their voices grew higher and higher.

Joshua, who had been sitting on the opposite side of the room on the couch, sprang up quickly and screamed back, "Everything

I have now, I have worked for. Nobody gave me any of it. How dare you call me spoiled!"

The fight seemed to last all night but in actuality, it may have been around half an hour. As it began, I jumped from the couch and ran towards them screaming to stop. They were wrapped in a tight embrace hitting each other, rolling over furniture, and breaking things. In fear, and in need of help, I ran to the neighbor's house and told her to call the police. She didn't even question me but said okay and had the phone in her hand right away. I ran back into the house to try and stop the fight. Papi, feeling disrespected by Joshua, would not let up on him. But Joshua was no longer a kid, he was a twenty-two-year-old man and was fed up with the years of mistreatment from Papi. I could see the years of hurt and frustration in my brother's eyes.

I heard Papi tell my brother to get out and my anxiety hit full swing. As Joshua walked downstairs to his room to get his stuff, I pleaded in tears with Papi to leave him alone, but my begging fell on deaf ears. Papi followed Joshua downstairs and continued the fight. Now, here is where a scary situation became a little comical. I grew up watching shows like Sanford and Son, so I had seen the character Fred call out to his dead wife saying he's having a heart attack. I was willing to try anything I guess, so I put my hands over my chest and shouted, "Oh, my heart! My heart!" I am truly Abuelita's granddaughter because she did the same thing when she wanted to diffuse intense situations!

But of course, they didn't notice my antics. Joshua pinned Papi down and was about to deliver a knock-out blow when I screamed, "Joshua, no! Remember Jesus!" At that, he stopped fist in mid-air. He was looking down at Papi with hurt and anger on his face.

Papi's anger seemed to leave him instantly at the fact that Joshua was bleeding from his head. Suddenly he was truly concerned for his son's well-being. He calmly said to Joshua, "Breathe, son, breathe."

The police arrived and talked to Papi, but my brother had already left the house to try to walk himself into a calmer state. I was torn between the choice of staying with Papi, who was being put in handcuffs or going after my brother, Joshua. Although I hated to leave Papi, I felt Joshua needed me more. With socks on my feet and charged with emotions, I ran into the night looking for my brother. When I found him, I pleaded for him to come home. He was very angry and was walking fast but I eventually was able to persuade him to come home where an ambulance was waiting.

At first, he didn't want to get into the ambulance because he was afraid of the cost.

"Do we have insurance? How much is this going to cost?" he asked me.

"Don't worry about it, just go and let them help you. I'll be right behind you to the hospital."

I convinced Joshua to go to the hospital where I would meet him. I got into my Pontiac Sunfire and followed right behind the ambulance, praying all the way to the hospital. At the hospital, Joshua received two stitches for his head wound. We talked for a while as he sat up in the hospital bed with me at his side. He admitted that he had already forgiven Papi. He told me that what snapped him out of his anger and brought him back to reality was when I said

"Jesus."

We started joking around afterward. There was a box of clean hospital rags by his bed, and he told me to take them home saying how much I loved to clean. I did grab some and we both laughed. It was nice to have such an intense situation finally diffused. Laughter always does that. It's funny how much it saved us over the years from suffering the intensity of the hardships in our house.

Papi was taken to the local detention center but was released the following day. I told him to call me and I would pick him up but he never did. Maybe he needed the time to think.

The next morning, he was already home in the kitchen talking to Mary. She later told me that he walked home about fourteen miles without a coat in the cold. It hurt me to think about him going through that. She also told me that Papi cried in the kitchen while telling her what happened. I wondered about how that made her feel because I had never seen Papi cry. I can't picture it even now and yet my heart breaks at the thought.

Joshua ended up moving in with his boss's family who treated him kindly. Mami, who had been at work when this happened, was heartbroken and torn.

As for me, Papi told me that he would never forgive me for getting the police involved. He felt humiliated being led away in front of the neighbors that night, but I knew I had done the right thing. I was afraid someone was going to die that night. I was determined to stop death from entering our front door no matter what the cost.

Because of the domestic situation at my house that evening, Papi had to get a lawyer. I was to be a witness and testify to what happened. I was on the side of the state which meant I was against Papi. It also didn't help that Joshua was leaving for the Air Force in a few weeks and we were all afraid that this would keep him from going. Around this same time, our beloved Abuelita had a massive stroke, and her memory was affected.

Meanwhile, graduation from college loomed and my grades continued to drop. I was having a hard time trying to balance my emotions which were all over the place. Finally, it was time to talk to Papi's lawyer about what happened. I drove to his office wondering what to expect and how I would handle all my emotions. Anxiety-ridden and nervous, I walked into the office prepared to tell the truth, hoping it wouldn't hurt Papi. I met with the lawyer and answered his questions, recounting the whole fight. I began to cry when I recanted all that happened that night.

The lawyer was very sympathetic to me and thankful for my testimony. I never had to go into a courtroom, thank God. I don't think I would have survived speaking against my father to save my brother. I loved them both.

After speaking with the lawyer, it was finally over. Joshua entered the Air Force without any problems. I breathed a sigh of relief. No more of those two fighting now—they were both safe.

But I couldn't deal with living with Papi anymore. The emotional roller coaster was too intense. It was time to start thinking about my departure from the house as well.

Poetry
by Maritza

Dark Side #1

I can't see you but I feel you.
I always know you're there.
You never fail me.
But you've got nowhere to go
So, of course, you're here with me.
Stuck to me like glue.
I am your life's force.
I am the only source
To your outside world
That I allow to unfurl.
So, you can touch reality
To show all your ability
In bringing me so low,
My pain, you thrive to show,
You cut me down so quickly
And embarrass me so sickly
In presenting my vulnerability
To all who watch intently
To see my next move
To see what I can prove.
But all I do is sit there
All of my insides spread out everywhere.
I look up at you to stop.
You just smile at me and pop!
I'm okay again cause
I took my medicine
And you're back on the bottom of my shoe
Until we can do it again.

Out of the Darkness

I stand alone, or so I think
Emptiness surrounding me
Nothingness
Bleak and obscure
I look to find direction
But if there were arrows, they'd lead nowhere

At first, there is no sound
Only the faint beat of my heart
It starts to grow louder
Until the deafening sound brings me to my knees

I clasp my hands together and I pray
I pray for another day
I wish the darkness to end
To be taken out of this misery
Yet I want to live

Trapped inside my own mind
Taunted by my own failures
Why is this happening again?
It grows stronger and quicker
Faster and broader
Again, and again until I feel like I
Can take no more
And then...

The sun rises
I've made it thru
The light filters out everything
I am still here

And I can see again.

Adrenaline

Your laugh is wicked, high pitched and wretched
I have sent you away into oblivion before
Yet again you stand at my door
Scratching with your claws ever so
Slightly, annoyingly, irritatingly

Drawing me in just to the brink so that
I can let you in
There is no sight, everything drowns in colors
Sound seems obsolete

There's only feeling, there is only you and me
You anchor into me as if I were a host
And you suck the breath out of me
But I have disclosed my secret weapon
I shine it on you like a flashlight

And you wither and decay like a rose
That has gone without sun and water
You fall back into your pit
And the chains clasp hungrily at your
Ankles and wrists

Dare to escape again?
Do you have the strength?
I no longer have the desire to taunt you
And you will no longer taunt me.

Hunger

Hello out there!
Can you hear me?
Can't you feel me?
Stop running!
Stop walking!
Stop working and recharge, replenish then resume.

I am a reminder of your humanity.
Take notice of me!
There are those who can't think nothing else but me
Yet you run as if air were your fuel!

You will dwindle and I will become stronger
I don't understand weight
I don't understand fashion
I only know when I am in need
And you can do nothing if you don't heed

But make you miserable and give you pain
Take care of me and I will take care of you
You do not lack what is needed
As others do
So feed me!

Brain

I am haggard
Do you not rest?
Even as you sleep, you think
Oh, I wish I could take a vacation from you!
But my place is here
And I am entrusted with your memories
Your actions, your life.
So how can I leave?
You need me.
And I do not fault you for that
Yet I am fried
I try to tell you through
Blurred vision and aches.
Rest
And my great power shall be your reward.
These thoughts and plans you make
Run through me like a freight train.
I can decipher it all
But I shouldn't have to
Not at that speed.

Bloom

Why can't you tell them what needs to be said?
Why do you hold it in?
Why do you hesitate and get intimidated?
What's the worst that they can do, say no?
Well, you can say no too.
Stand on your two feet dammit!
Use your voice!
This has gone on too long!
What's the matter.........?

Oh hon, I'm sorry.
I'm being too hard on you again.
It's just that I get so frustrated!
Why do you insist on being ordinary?
Is it because it's safe?

Well, you were never meant to be that.
It's not part of your makeup.
You are meant to bloom.
Everyone expects more of you.
We all see your potential.
So, show the world what you can do!

Pest

What the…?
Who's there?
What do you want?
You evil pest, go away!
I can stand you no longer!
Bug someone else!
Go bug the wall.
Now there's a task for you.
But leave me alone.
I have outgrown you.
Run along
Or I'll hit you.

Stuck

There are times when I feel stuck
Don't know which way to turn or what's what
I wish that I could do more than just enough
But I'm stuck with these thoughts that won't set me free

Sometimes I lie awake for hours
I think about what could be and what hasn't been and I
Try to fall asleep just to forget
That my dreams are dead and I'm
Stuck in my head so I...

Chorus:
Try to move on try to hold on
But I don't even know what to hold on to
I'm trapped in this hopelessness
I try to cheer up try to believe that this is just
Temporary
But time keeps on moving and nothing has changed

People try to say that it's okay
And they try to make me feel better, but I
Can't seem to leave this empty space
And I don't know what to do anymore so I…

Chorus (Repeat)

Bridge:
Nothing's gonna change unless I change it myself
All I need is faith the size of a mustard seed
And when I reach out His hand will steady me
It's not too late for me to believe so I

Know I'll move on and keep holding on
And in one moment I'll see that His grace is
All that I will ever need

Burdened But Thankful

You exhaust me
You bring me fear, almost to my knees
You have me
Or do you?

You make me feel unworthy
You have me searching the eyes of all I meet
Looking, looking for validation
Am I ok?
Can someone please tell me that I'm, ok?

And through the fits and panic spells
I'm still anchored
Every fearful thought that makes me
Believe I've reached the point of no return
Still, finds me anchored.

You make me feel like I am not enough
Yet you make me great just the same
The fear and the dark days are replaced
By an undying strength.

You knock me down just to give me the
Strength to rise up again.

It's you that I am burdened, but thankful.

You shut the sun out from my eyes just to draw back the
Shades again.
You push me firm into the mud
Just to pick me up again.
Are you my curse or my blessing?

You separate me from life just
To connect me again with more desire.
You pierce my heart just to make
Whole my soul again.

You rob me of smiles just
To bring me laughter.
You make me who I am.

I am burdened but thankful.

Because of you I lead others.
Because of you, I love with a
Deep unending love.
Because of you I'm fiercely
Independent.

And that is why, though I may be
Undeniably, miserably, hopelessly,
Unquestionably burdened,
I am thankful.

Chapter Thirteen
Failure and Success

Close to the end of my senior year in college, the talk about a course called Field Camp came up among my classmates. Some had already gone or were applying and after thinking about it, I felt I was ready, so I applied. Field Camp is a master's or graduate course where you travel with a group of students to a location (domestically or internationally) to study rock formations and learn how to map them. Many universities offer this course in their Geology departments for those planning to obtain a Master's of Geology.

I went online and found a university in Buffalo, New York that was taking students for four weeks to Utah, Wyoming, and Colorado. Most Field Camp courses were six weeks in length and I wasn't sure I could go that long so when I found one for less time, I jumped at it. I had always wanted to go to those states, so I applied and paid my down payment for the trip. I bought all of my camping equipment (Mami bought me a sleeping bag for Christmas) and was ready to go. I would be flying into Colorado to meet with my new classmates. I had been thinking about the trip for weeks and I felt I was ready. I was hopeful that the confidence I had obtained over the years of accomplishing small, independent tasks would lead me on this new adventure.

Departure day finally arrived and I started to get butterflies in my stomach. Mami drove me to the airport, but on the way there my confidence began to drop as I allowed the unknown to produce that familiar fearful feeling. The light, cooling effects of the adrenaline began to creep up my arms as doubt increased in my head. I began to cry. How could I ever think I could do this? Fly by myself halfway across the country to spend four weeks with strangers? I'm nuts!

"What's wrong, Flaca?" Mami asked as she drove us onto the exit ramp towards the airport.

"I feel like I am at a crossroads."

"What do you mean?" she asked again.

"If I go, I don't know if I'll have a panic attack and get worse. I don't know what to expect, and that scares me. But if I stay, I'm afraid I'll fall into a deep depression. I'm scared either way."

"What do you want to do?"

"I don't know. I don't want to feel this way. I want to have my life back. I hate being so afraid!" I cried, tears streaming down my face. I felt like I was failing myself all over again. I had bought all the stuff and paid all the dues but deep down, I knew I wouldn't be going.

"It's okay, whatever you decide. But I think once you get on the plane, you'll be fine."

The fear once again began to overwhelm me. I wondered, what am I to expect out there? What if I get lost? What if I have a panic attack and can't come home?

We arrived at the airport, and I stepped up to the check-in counter and immediately froze.

"Miss? Your bags please?"

I just couldn't do it. Racked with nerves, scared out of my head, I turned around toward Mami and walked away from the counter. Mami was understanding, as always, but sad for me. She tried to encourage me to get on the plane, reminding me that once I faced my fears, I would be okay. But I had already made up my mind. I was running away. I didn't trust that I would actually have a good time and keep my anxieties at bay.

I found a bench in the lobby and collapsed in tears. I phoned Kaitlyn, another Geology student whom I had met in one of my core courses. She had gone on the same trip before and knew all about it. I explained to her what had happened. Sympathetic to my situation, she too encouraged me to make the trip regardless of my fears, but I was too afraid. I was not ready to leave my comfort zone.

"I know you can do it, Maritza," she said. "You will have a great time! Just walk over to the counter. I believe in you. I know you can do it."

Kaitlyn had gone to Field Camp and met the love of her life! Why was it so hard for me? "That's just it though, Kait. I don't know if I can do it. I just can't seem to put one foot in front of the other this time." I wept. I now knew in the pit of my stomach this trip was not going to happen. Nothing anyone could say could make the feelings go away. I'd given in to the anxiety and panicky feelings as I'd always done in the past—like the trip to Texas to see Javier that I never took, fearful of what could happen.

Kaitlyn listened and was sympathetic as always. She was also sad that I was having such a hard time. After getting off the phone with her I told Mami, "Let's go home." We walked back to our parked van and put all my stuff back in and Mami drove us home. Anxiety and nervousness had won again. I had become so obsessed with anticipating what could happen in the future that I scared myself away from something that could have been great and robbed myself of the present. Standing in that airport, steps away from a wonderful adventure, I talked myself out of it once again.

I waited for the depression to come but another emotion came surprisingly in its place—relief. I was even laughing with Mami about stopping at Walmart on the way home. The depression truly never came. It made me wonder if it was not the right time for me to go to Field Camp. *Well, this is odd. Where is the normal depression that always follows my fear and anxiety? It's usually like an equation or recipe. The outcome is always the same when you put the first two ingredients together. But not this time.*

For days and weeks after, I wondered what could have been if I wasn't so filled with anxiety.

I wrote a letter in great detail describing my actions to the professor who was leading the University of Buffalo Field Camp course. I explained why I was not going to make it on the trip. I had thought about lying because I was afraid of what he might think, but in the end, I told the truth and received a refund. Telling the truth to someone I had never met except through emails about having panic attacks felt freeing to me. I figured, after all, the professor was a person, too—we're all human.

After that, I wrote another email to my professors explaining I would be coming back to finish my courses and would not be going to Field Camp as planned. You can imagine the embarrassment I felt. Everyone at school knew I had planned on going. I realized there was nothing to say. I was tired of lying and making up excuses just to please other people and hiding what was going on with me. Thankfully, they were very respectful and didn't ask me any questions and I was able to get back to my studies easily.

At school, I got right back to my work. I began my senior research project with one of my professors and decided to throw myself into this final assignment hoping to forget about what happened with Field Camp. My project consisted of proving the era or timeline of some rock specimens from the upper portion of the Appalachian Mountains. My samples came from a town called New Baltimore, PA. Little did I know that years later, my life would be changed forever not far from that town.

I put together a large poster with a map of the Appalachian Belt, where my samples came from, along with pictures of their thin sections. Thin sections are very thin slices of rock in which the minerals and crystals in them could be seen under a special microscope. At the end of my research, I was then to give a presentation on my findings in front of the professors who taught in the Geosciences Department and also my peers. The presentation part scared me because I struggled so hard to understand what I was putting together. Despite my studies, I felt that I still lacked knowledge. All I knew was that I loved the subject.

The day came when each classmate would give a presentation on his or her senior research project. Stepping into the light of the projector and turning to face everyone, I prayed not only for grace to get through my presentation but that it would go well. My insides were shaking as I fought back thoughts of another panic attack.

"Welcome everyone," I started. "Today, I will be presenting my research on The Geologic Character of the Former Upper Devonian Appalachian Mountain Belt." I know, sounds pretty smart, huh? Ah, don't feel intimidated, all of us Geology folks are just rock heads.

I did my best. I don't remember it being a long presentation. I had some questions at the end and answered them as best I could. It was over and I didn't die! Stupid anxiety! I'm still here.

After that semester, I was finally graduating from college, and it was the happiest day of my life! Throughout the years of fear, panic attacks, depression, and sorrow, I'd cried many times in frustration wondering if I'd ever get through school. I had so much other stuff filling my head that often it was difficult to attend classes, concentrate on lectures, retain information, or do homework.

But God knew how much I wanted to graduate and how hard I had worked to push through the struggles of my anxiety and depression. He knew all the times I had begged the University to allow me to continue to the next semester when they wanted to put me on academic probation for my low GPA. He knew how horrible I felt when I failed a class and when I couldn't focus on the work because of my nervousness. He knew the countless exams I failed because I could not retain the information I'd studied. And He knew how I struggled with telling myself I was smart and not stupid. I prayed relentlessly. He knew all of it because He was there through it all—by my side.

Please, please let me pass! Make it stick in my brain. Help me, God, please! Help me to stay, to finish. I just want to finish! Please, please God, please, I pleaded. Many, many prayers like this I prayed repeatedly during my years at school. I couldn't give up because I believed if I did, even if I took off a semester, I wouldn't finish school. God pulled me through the muck of my ongoing battle by reassuring me that I deserved my degree.

Graduation day finally arrived. It was a beautiful, sunny day without a cloud in the great blue sky. The college stadium was vast and spacious. I had never attended a game the entire time I went to college so being there was a first for me. I wore a pink knee-length dress with white flowers underneath my gown. Kaitlyn let me borrow her cap and gown so I wouldn't have to buy one, and I was grateful.

My group of graduates and I stood at the edge of the football field in the grass waiting to go to our seats. My heels dug into the soft earth, and I regretted my decision to wear them. Mami and my sisters, Ariana and Mary, sat in the stands cheering me on as my group was given the 'go ahead' signal to move forward. We marched to our seats in groups. Then it hit me. I was graduating!

I reached my seat and sat down and began surveying the area. Anxiety started to bite at me as I noticed how many seats and rows there were. *This whole thing is gonna take forever! Will I be able to sit here and go through it without freaking out and having to leave in front of everyone? The fact that we needed to remain seated until our names were called was enough for my heart to begin pounding.* The thought of any loss of control on my part created a sliver of fear that raced down my spine like a chill. *Oh control, control. You sneaky thing, you. Does anybody have a good hold on you?*

I couldn't get up and leave as I did in a classroom or church using the bathroom as an excuse when the feelings started. Sitting in the middle of a stadium filled with people I felt every eye on me. *No. You're not going to take this from me. Not today!* I began to breathe slowly and soon, I started to relax. Presently, the naming of the graduates began. When the motion was given for my row, I stood up with the rest and marched head high towards the stage. *It's finally happening! I'm going to be okay.* As long as I was moving, I knew I was good.

The lady signaled me over from where I waited at the edge of the stage. I walked up to her hoping not to trip and handed her my card with my name on it. She called my name and the department I was graduating from and handed me my degree saying, "Congratulations." I don't even remember her face or how she sounded. Receiving my degree occurred in seconds. I turned for a photo and then walked to the other end of the stage and back down the steps and towards my seat. That was it, but it was more than enough. I held that piece of paper tightly. I returned to my seat with all the confidence in the world at that moment. I did it! I've earned this degree and nothing or nobody can take that away from me. *I'm proud of you, Maritza.* I smiled to myself.

Chapter Fourteen
Living on the Edge

After college, I went to work for a geotechnical company in Harford County, Maryland, and finally moved into my own place. I worked as a Soils Technician/Inspector in construction materials testing and observation. This is where I developed the skills that would propel me into the career that I have today as a Public Works Inspector III for the Department of Transportation of Baltimore City.

I enjoyed working there at that first job out of school and met some pretty awesome people including my good friend, Tanya. She was funny, easy to talk to, and very spiritual. She spoke about her love for Christ and all He had done for her. It became very easy for me to share my burden of anxiety with her, and we often prayed for each other together. I found comfort in having a Christian friend so close to me that I could go to for spiritual guidance and speak in confidence. She was a single mother to a young son and very confident in whom God made her to be. She taught me to be confident and reminded me that God is for us and never against us. This brought me comfort.

Having a confidante made it easier for me to share another part of myself that I still kept secret—my singing. I began writing songs in English and Spanish around age fifteen, before my anxiety robbed me of my confidence, and had written one called "Moved On" about a crush I had. One day on the job site, feeling comfortable about it, I sang it for Tanya just the first verse and the chorus.

"That was really nice. You're good Maritza. I feel there is more in there."

I felt my face flush. Maybe, just maybe I should start singing again, I thought.

One day, my office manager announced she was searching for someone to sing the National Anthem at the company picnic that was going to take place at a local minor league baseball field. It took me days to muster up the courage to volunteer.

Just do it, Maritza. They aren't even asking for auditions. This is what you love to do. You never know unless you try. Oh, how I wanted to sing but I was still so afraid.

Finally, I walked into my manager's office and asked if they were still looking for someone to sing. He said yes and right there and then I said I would do it! He was surprised because, again, no one knew I sang except for Tanya.

It was a beautiful summer day and the sky was clear. I arrived early at the stadium. There weren't many people there by the time I was called up to sing for which I was grateful! The announcer called my name, and I walked up to home plate where the microphone stood, and did my thing. Nervous and a little shaky, I started slow, enunciating each word and using my head voice. I remembered to breathe but didn't belt the song out because I was too aware of the mic, and I wanted my voice to carry through just right. As I closed on the song, a sense of accomplishment washed over me, and I was glad it was over. The audience clapped, and afterward, the minor league team took the field. I even got a compliment from an associate from another office.

"Well done, Maritza. That was very nice."

"Thank you!" I said excitedly.

As the day went on, more people came to the picnic. I was having fun, relaxed, and proud of myself. Midway through the event, the National Anthem was to be sung again which confused me. There were more people in the stands and the minor league team was about to go out again. I guess the game they'd played after I sang was just a warmup. Another singer belted out the song and received many cheers including one from Tanya.

"Go'head girl," she said as the singer ended with a grand finish.

Immediately any trace of confidence I had died after hearing the other singer's velvety deep voice followed by the huge applause. Once again, my singing days were over.

It was around this time when Mami was promoted to a managerial position for the Internal Revenue Service in Virginia. She had come from the Baltimore office and was just filling in at the Virginia office until the office could find a replacement. The promotion would require her and Ariana to move to Virginia permanently, which meant my parents would be splitting up again. Ariana was still in high school at the time. My brothers, Ezra and Joshua were serving in the United States Air Force. Mary and I lived together in an apartment in town. Mami had grown tired of the constant fighting with Papi and how nothing had changed after they got back together years earlier. When she first started to fill in for the job, I asked if there was a chance it could lead to a permanent position.

"Do you think they will ask you to take the job?" I asked.

"No. I am only there temporarily until they find a manager for that office. I doubt they would offer the position to me," she replied.

Well, the Virginia office did offer the position to Mami. She saw it as not only an opportunity to grow in her job but as God giving her another chance to be happy. The relationship between my parents had continued to deteriorate and Mami felt that she needed a change. This position came at the right time and made the decision for a life change much easier for her. The fighting was never going to stop. My parents couldn't live together happily.

"They're giving me the position," she soon announced.

"You, see? I knew it! I'm happy for you Mami." And I really was. I knew that this could happen. Deep down, I knew. But it meant she would be moving three hours away from me and I could not just stop by and see her whenever I wanted. For a while, I told myself that I was okay with the change. But here's the thing about anxious people—change is almost never easy.

Soon I began to have anxious moments at work brought on by self-doubt. Could I make it without Mami nearby? How was I going to be there for myself? Could I even trust myself? She was my support, my backbone. Am I going to be strong enough to be there for myself when the bottom falls out?

This triggered another bout of depression in my life. I was sad more times than I was happy. I struggled with my thoughts and emotions, feeling that no one knew what I was going through. I felt alone and that I needed to shape up—that I needed to fight. But I was so tired all the time. I tried so hard to combat the coming anxiety. It's emotionally exhausting and devastating to know that something horrible is coming and you feel unable to stop it. It's like a cold, rough blanket that covers you and you feel uncomfortable but can't remove it. Then the familiar cycle began—waking up with nervousness and nausea, dry heaving in the bathroom sink, being unable to eat, and missing work. It never happened right away but gradually, over time.

Chapter Fifteen
Missing in Action

One morning while driving to another job site, I began to have a panic attack. It first hit me when I realized that I hadn't eaten anything for breakfast. I had become very strict about eating three square meals a day since I was always concerned about losing weight. In my car, I started to worry about the fact that I had skipped breakfast and it was already eleven a.m.

The panic attack began with the cold rush of adrenaline running down my arms and back. My stomach was doing somersaults. I felt cold but was sweating as if I were hot. It had been a while since the last attack, so when this one came, I was shaken to my core. The adrenaline rush I was experiencing scared me to death. My mind began to race, and I instantly wanted to be home. I wanted to run away but the fact that I was still at work and needed to be responsible made the attack worse. My Aunt Lucy called me while I was driving, but I couldn't even stay on the phone to talk to her because I was in panic mode. (Of course, I didn't tell her that!) Later I wondered if God told her to call and distract me from my panicky thoughts, but I didn't get the hint.

I arrived at the job site and could still feel the onslaught of raw emotion. It was like hitting a brick wall at a hundred and fifty miles an hour. I met Tanya at the job site, and right away she could tell something was wrong.

"What's wrong?" she asked.

"I'm having a panic attack. I don't feel well. I don't think I can stay."

"Just calm down. It's gonna be okay. I think you should stay."

She was right. If I had stayed, I would have felt better. But I had already decided I was too scared to continue working and that I needed to go home. I didn't have the confidence to stay and finish the rest of the day. I ended up giving her my working equipment so that I wouldn't have to take it back to the office.

"Can you take the gauge back with you, please?"

"Yeah, sure. No problem. You gonna be okay?" she asked.

"Yeah, I just need to get home." I couldn't risk anyone else seeing the state I was in. I needed to leave fast. It's as if I was trying to outrun the panic attack.

I was exhausted and now worried again about not having the strength to drive home. My boss, Bill, called me to tell me to go to another job site, but I told him that I was very sick and needed to rest.

The panic attack suddenly made me incapable of working.

I cursed the Devil because I felt that he was doing this to me for sport. He knew how much I was relying on God and praying. I felt that this panic attack was the Devil's way of unleashing his hatred upon me. In my mind, I had to run far away from the attack, but in reality, I knew that it was useless to run. Retreating to my comfort zone was the only way I could get a little peace.

I didn't even make it to my apartment. I was closer to Papi's house so I went there instead. For the next two weeks, I stayed at his house, calling out from work daily, trying to eat and sleep. My panic attack in the car that lasted ten minutes had grown into a sickness that would last several days. I spent those days living in fear of the next panic attack. I became immobilized from fear, and soon, the depression came and then snowballed. My negative self-talk only made things worse and my thoughts began to swirl in my head. *Why would I have a panic attack when everything was going so well? What's wrong with me? What is going on? This depression ruins everything! I hate this so much!* The depression had opened the door for negative thoughts, even thoughts of suicide, to spiral out of control in my mind.

I felt the need to explain to my boss what was going on with me. I kept calling out of work and he deserved an explanation. I went out on the front porch and sat on Papi's swinging bench to prepare for the call. I tried to gather my thoughts as the butterflies jumped inside my stomach. It felt more like they were slamming into one another—actually bats, not butterflies. Nervous and not knowing what to expect, I called him and told him the truth about my state of being and dangerous thoughts.

"Hey Bill, I'm...I'm so sorry to be missing work. I've been going through something pretty bad," I said. My thoughts started to run. *Just tell him the truth, don't lie. He's a nice boss, maybe he'll understand.* I swallowed hard, then I just let the words fall out.

"I, uh, suffer from depression and I've been battling thoughts of suicide," I confessed.

Bill was very patient and compassionate with me. He listened intently and didn't interrupt.

"Maritza, I had no idea. Listen, just take some time for yourself. I'll put you in for vacation. Just communicate with me about what's going on so that I know if I can put you on the schedule at work. Please take care of yourself."

"Thank you so much, Bill," I said in tears. We ended the call, and I sent a thankful prayer to God for Bill's understanding.

Because of Bill's compassion, I was able to pay my rent and bills using the vacation time he approved for me. I believed God intervened through my boss for my finances. They were the last thing I needed to worry about.

After a couple of weeks at Papi's, I went back to my apartment. Ariana, who was thirteen at the time, came to visit. At the time, Mami was still transitioning to the Virginia office so Ariana was finishing up school in Maryland and living with Papi while Mami came back and forth. One morning as I lay in bed, my mind began to rush with negative thoughts. I shot straight up and pulled my legs over the side of the bed. *You're gonna lose your job. You will never get better and will be stuck like this forever. There's no escape.*

The adrenaline started as I began to believe the thoughts. Fear raced through me, and I was too exhausted this time to try to stop it. Not eating well again because of the nervousness, I was light-headed and weak. *This is your life. You are not strong enough to fight this. You can't control your own mind. God, Stop this! Stop this, please! I need peace. I gotta do something. I can't do this anymore...*

I was also afraid because Ariana was in the apartment with me and would notice how bad I was feeling. I couldn't even count on the bliss of sleep that I was able to depend on in the past. The thoughts wouldn't stop. Then, the image of a knife came into my mind. I had one in the kitchen drawer. I saw myself turning my left wrist upward and holding the knife in my other hand. I thought to myself, do it. *Do it. The pain will stop. Just do it. You're a good girl, you'll go to heaven. It's okay. Do it. DO IT!*

I was paralyzed by these thoughts. *I can't! Not if Ariana is here! What am I going to do? I can't do that to her!* I was weary physically and mentally. Completely drained from the depression and the obsessive scary thoughts, I felt hopeless. The thoughts of ending it all also scared me because I had been taught in my Christian faith that suicide was a mortal sin, and I would go straight to hell if I killed myself. I surely didn't want that, but a part of me didn't want to live either so I was trapped.

Knowing sweet Ariana was in the next room without any idea of what was happening, I realized I couldn't pull off such a gruesome act in front of her, and in my moment of despair, in that black, airless hole, an intervention appeared. All of a sudden, I heard a knock at the front door. The noise startled me and, in a dash, I rushed to my bedroom window and peered through. I was stunned to see Papi standing outside of my apartment.

I was shocked Papi had stopped by unannounced because I'd told him not to come to my home earlier in the year if he was going to vent to me about all his problems. He did that a lot and it would trigger my depressive thoughts. He would stop by to fight and argue rather than visit. When I was dealing with depression, I didn't have enough emotional energy to deal with what was bothering him. I had explained to him that my apartment was a place of peace, and if he was going to come to fight, then he should not come at all.

For a long time, he had obeyed my wishes and had stopped coming by my apartment. This day, however, while I was struggling with thoughts of suicide, Papi did show up, unannounced, in my worst moment. Rather than get mad at him, I realized this was another gift from God and I was grateful. *Oh, my goodness, thank You, Jesus! Thank You so much!*

I hastily packed a bag and ran to the living room where Ariana was watching TV and said, "We're leaving!"

"What? Why? Can't we stay here?" she asked.

"No, we're going with Papi. Get your stuff."

She rolled her eyes and I knew it was because she didn't want to be at the house with him. But she didn't know how badly I needed this.

Papi took Ariana and me back to his house without any question and he took care of us both. At Papi's house, I slowly got through the anxiety. Papi liked taking care of me which took my mind off taking care of myself. I began to feel safe again and I was very grateful for him, even though he never realized what was really happening. Just like the gentleman customer in Target who came at my lowest moment to tell me that I had value, God intervened with Papi. God knew I needed help and He saved me again—this time, through my father.

I never told Papi what he did for me meant so much then, and that it still does. Despite all of the past fighting, Papi was there for me in my hour of need and I will never forget that.

I remember hearing somewhere that God can use anyone to do His will here on earth. God knew my desperation and sent Papi, the one person whom I felt had always shunned God. For me, this was an example of His omnipotence.

Eventually, I returned to work and was assigned lighter tasks, for which I was grateful since I was only beginning to get my strength back. I started eating light foods that I could get down, like yogurt and soup, until my appetite returned. I resumed seeing my psychiatrist with whom I would share everything that had happened to me. I knew I had to keep going to work, had to keep living.

During my recovery period, I would write poems about how I was feeling and that seemed to help. Most importantly, during this time, I realized again that God would not let me go. I kept trying to regain strength and a normal routine one day at a time. Soon, I was back to my old self…at least for the time being.

Chapter Sixteen
The Icy Hill

The opportunity for another trip arrived and for the third time, I failed to get on a plane due to fear.

Mary and I were supposed to travel to Puerto Rico for a family reunion. Mami, Ariana were already there. It had been years since our family had all been together; even Ezra and Joshua, who had previously been unable to go while in the service, were there.

Out of his huge, generous heart and knowing how important it was for me to be with my family, my Uncle Tony paid for the airplane tickets for Mary and me. I was excited for us to meet up with Mami, Ariana, and the boys, and see the rest of our family. Yet like clockwork, I started to feel very nervous about the flight the closer the day came to leave.

That morning, as Mary drove us to the airport, my anxiety turned into a full-blown panic attack. We were supposed to fly out of Washington D. C., and we got lost in the city. I started sweating, shaking, and dry heaving. She had to pull over for me because I felt the need to throw up. I opened the door and stuck my head out and down towards the pavement, but nothing came out. After that, I asked her to drive me back home. I remember being so tired from the attack that I slept all the way home—but that didn't free me from the guilt I felt at her missing the flight because of me.

After she dropped me off, she returned to the airport and was able to board another flight. I stayed home. I was glad that I didn't hinder her from making the trip, but I was deeply saddened that I didn't go. My whole family was there, and I was home. I felt disappointed in myself. This pattern of not going on flights because of the fear of panic attacks created another prison for me. *Will I ever fly again?*

I called Tanya, who also doesn't like getting on planes, and we talked for a while.

"What's up my Puerto Rican praline?" she said, cheerfully. Tanya and I have cute nicknames for each other. Mine for her was "Chocolate Lava Cake."

"I feel awful. I was supposed to go on a trip to Puerto Rico, but I couldn't get on the plane. We didn't even make it to the airport before Mary took me back home." I replied sadly.

"Girl, you know I hate planes too. But you know what? We can salvage this day. Come out to Havre de Grace with me and we can sit outside and talk Mary Kay, sound good?"

Tanya sold Mary Kay cosmetics and at one point I did too. I agreed and we hung up. I got up, got dressed, and got in the car. *Don't you feel sorry for yourself! You made your decision, so let it go now and enjoy this day.* We met up in Havre de Grace and sat outside her grandmother's house, enjoying the beautiful sunny day.

I was and am very grateful to her for getting me out of my apartment. If I had stayed, I would have wallowed in self-pity and depression all weekend. That would not have set me up to have a good week ahead. Because of her support and encouragement, the sickness and depression didn't have a chance to take over. I was out in the fresh air with things on my mind other than myself. A good support system is a gift during hard times. *Remember, one foot in front of the other. Don't stop...*

During my constant battle with anxiety and depression, I experienced more relapses than I care to admit. All the missed opportunities due to my fear of what could happen left me feeling my life would be one setback after another. I became increasingly frustrated and disappointed with myself. My therapist compared relapse to driving up an icy hill in a car, wheels spinning. Every time you try to shoot straight up, you slide back down to the bottom of the hill.

"Think of it like this. Have you ever tried to drive straight up an icy hill? What happens? The back tires spin, right? The easiest way to get to the top of a hill like that is slowly driving in a zigzag pattern until you reach the top. It takes time but you will get there. Fake it 'til you make it!" he said.

He painted such a vivid picture that it made it easier to understand that dealing with my fears was going to take some time and patience. In my bouts of depression and anxiety, I wanted to get better lightning fast, not taking the time to be patient with the process. I kept finding myself spinning my tires and sliding back down the icy hill of my struggle. I did this countless times until I became so depressed, so exhausted I lay there at the bottom, in the dark, freezing, cold. I wasn't learning from my mistakes. But depression can make it hard to retain information, too.

Keeping busy helped, when I had energy, but the depression would cause me to become so unmotivated all I wanted to do was sleep after work and on the weekends. I stopped going to the gym and taking the voice lessons I had begun earlier in the year, to bring singing back into my life.

I wanted to move forward with my dream of singing and performing. But I stopped writing songs and poems because I was not getting the results I wanted when I wanted them. The creativity was drying up in me, leaving behind a desert.

> *Journal Entry: 11:03 pm, 1/6/04*
> *I know I need to be patient with my songwriting but why can't I find my creative side? And why do I let people go on about me, complimenting me and telling me how wonderful I am like how Miriam was doing the other day? I just don't feel worthy enough. I don't think I ever felt worthy enough. I guess when I start believing I am and that I've accomplished a lot maybe I won't feel so out of place. I figure I better loosen up or chill but then I feel miserable. I'm so lazy! If I chill anymore, I'll become immune to the ice caps of the earth! I'm a determined lazy person. Oh yes, the worst kind there is. In short, a dreamer! My singing has been put off 'til God knows when because I keep making excuses for it. I'm just not ready. The sad thing is I don't think I'm going to do it. I don't want to get stuck into the same routine! When am I gonna change this? I want to have it all. I want God to show me where I'm supposed to be! Are you showing me? Am I worthy of Your blood, God? Who am I?*

I was racing up that icy hill on bald tires and then slamming into the bottom every time.

I changed jobs in November of 2007 to further my career in construction inspections. I went to work for another geotechnical company in the Baltimore/Washington area. My supervisor was immediately impressed with how quickly I learned to work in each department as needed. When the company was awarded a government project that entailed the construction of nine buildings at a local military installation, I was the one they chose to lead the inspection part of it.

Knowing that my boss had confidence in me to do this highly complex job boosted my confidence, so I said yes to leading the project. In my mind, life was looking up. The job site was located only twenty minutes away from my apartment so I felt it was within my comfort zone and that I would be able to handle all that this job would require of me. In the new position, I would lead a team of technicians and we would inspect the construction work from the ground up, for the brand-new buildings.

Some of the inspections included foundations, utilities, steel, and concrete, fireproofing, construction of a new roadway, drainage, curbs, and sidewalks. The job would require me to supervise and track the hours worked by my team of technicians/inspectors and myself. In the contract between my company and the client (a group of four contractors that came together as a Joint Venture, or the JV), our services were budgeted to be performed within typical forty-hour weeks, but, in actuality, many more work hours were required.

The overtime and the overworking of my technicians often led to frustration from all involved parties. My responsibilities continued to expand as the job progressed, which resulted in me having to work overtime reviewing reports, compiling daily summaries, and filling in for any absent technicians. My title was Onsite Resident Manager.

During this two-year government project, my company acquired a satellite office near the job site so that I wouldn't have to drive back and forth to the Baltimore area. I became certified to break concrete cylinders that we molded for strength testing. Most of the buildings had about five floors so there was a lot of concrete for my technicians and me to test. There were times when I was breaking fifty to ninety concrete cylinders per day by myself at the satellite office while my technicians were onsite performing inspections on the government contract. Between my responsibilities at the job site and my company's satellite office, I also had to manage personnel issues, including keeping the peace at times between my technicians/inspectors, and contractors. I was becoming overloaded and overwhelmed by it all.

I would drag my sweaty, dirty self into the office every evening. One day, I simply slept out of exhaustion on the office carpet floor. I had already worked two hours past my original shift, and I was beat. After starting work at 7 a.m. and dealing with the responsibilities of the day, I didn't care where I was able to lay my head so long as I was able to rest.

That evening, as I rested on the dusty carpet for about twenty minutes after a long day at the job site, I heard the phone ring. A group from the JV invited me to hang out with them at a local restaurant. I appreciated the invitation and decided to go unwind and have a meal with them. When I arrived, most of the team was already there and motioned for me to sit with them. As we began to have normal chit-chat, their concern about my well-being came up and some of them began to talk to me about what they had noticed.

"Hey, Maritz, how ya' doing, hon? You look a little worn out. Everything goin' okay? I could talk to your boss for you. I think you may be overworking yourself," one said.

"Yeah, we see you running all over the site. Do you need help?" another asked.

"Thanks, guys. No, I'm fine. You don't need to talk to my boss. It's okay, I'm hanging. Thanks for your concern though." I appreciated their concern. I was running all over the place. But I figured, that's what a good worker does, right?

❋

Back on the job site one morning, feeling exhausted, I was surprised to see that both my immediate and regional supervisors had arrived for a site visit. I was not expecting to see them that day. They had come to see how things were going and to check the progress of the construction. I pulled up in my white pick-up to one of the buildings at the edge of the job site and noticed them walking out of it. They saw me and walked toward me and asked me how the project was going. Overwhelmed with work, I struggled to find the right words to answer their question. My voice broke and the tears began. I tried hard not to cry but it was too late—the floodgates had opened with that simple question. Tired, stressed, and now, entirely embarrassed, I confessed that I just couldn't do everything that was piling up on my plate. The site at that point had about two thousand workers; including multiple subcontractors such as electricians, dirt crews, pipe or utility crews, concrete crews, steel installation crews, plumbers, welders, and landscapers.

My job as the Resident Onsite Inspection Manager was to make sure every inch of that site was covered by myself and my team of five technicians/inspectors. The more the site grew with construction, the more inspections were needed. Multiple buildings were constructed at the same time. The project had a completion deadline of two years. In that short amount of time, nine buildings, acres of parking lots, all underground utilities, and landscaping had to be completed and the construction could not go ahead without passing inspections. It could be very overwhelming. At times I thrived on it, but now, I was running on empty.

My supervisors, in support of my situation, granted me a week off to recuperate. I was grateful and desperately needed it. For months I had been losing weight and not getting nearly enough sleep, due to the demands of the job and the stress I put on myself.

The week off gave me the rest that I needed. Little did I know that love was right around the corner.

Chapter Seventeen
Heartbreak

Just before I had taken the week off, I met someone who worked on the site as well. He was one of the contractors and sometimes his work would require inspections from me or my crew. His name was Jason and he was hilarious! He made me laugh every time he came around which attracted me to him. During my week off, we had time away from the site where we got to know each other better and grew to enjoy each other's company.

He was very different from anyone I had ever known—a tattooed, motorcycle man who lived a carefree and spontaneous life. Some might say he's a "bad boy," but I found him to be a refreshing change from the strict rules by which I had been living. He had a good heart and was charming and fun. I found myself quickly and easily falling in love.

We spent most of our evenings and weekends together. I loved riding on the back of his motorcycle hanging out together at either his house or my apartment. Because I hadn't dated anyone since Darren back in college, I'd forgotten what it was like to be with someone and be in love. We would go to bars and meet up with his friends and coworkers and I'd listen and laugh at their stories. We even went to a concert at a local dive bar where he got to see his favorite musician play. That Christmas, he came along with my sisters, Mami and I to New York and met my family there. It was then, sadly, that I began feeling the relationship would not last.

It came as an empty feeling in the pit of my stomach. One evening while having dinner at my cousin's house, one of their kids remarked on the tattoos on Jason's arm. Some of them were pretty grown-up stuff and when he asked Jason about what they meant, I noticed Jason laugh it off and lower his shirt sleeve. After he went outside to drink a beer, Mami mentioned that we should not be sleeping in the same bed together (we were staying at my cousin's in her guest room while Mami and my sisters stayed at my aunt's house during the trip) because we were not married. Although she liked Jason, she was concerned about the example I was showing young Ariana and I knew she was right.

In the eyes of Christ, the only bed I should be sleeping in was my husband's. While everyone was still talking at the table, I went to the bathroom and cried. I knew that I was giving into a life that was not for me being with Jason even though I loved him. Soon it began to hit me that our goals in life were vastly different. I knew I wanted to be married and have a family in my future. I was also active in the Church and my faith was very important to me. I wanted to share it with someone who was on the same page as I was.

Jason, from the start, expressed to me that he was not very spiritual. I could see us disagreeing on how to raise our children in the church if we ever did have any. I think we both hoped that he would have a change of heart. But in the end, he couldn't change the way he felt about what he didn't want, and I couldn't change the way I felt about what I did.

The Sunday before I was about to break up with him, I was on my knees praying, crying to God to let me keep him. God knew I was in love with him and that I was distressed about ending our relationship. I felt guilty for my feelings, as though my desire to stay with my boyfriend were somehow against God, but deep down in my soul, I knew that God didn't view things the way I did. I realized God wanted to show me He had other plans for both of us and each of our journeys would take us in different directions.

"I'm never gonna have what I want with Jason, huh, God?" I asked silently, as the tears flowed freely down my hot cheeks. On my knees, I placed my hands on my lap and lowered my head in sadness.

"Do You think You could help him desire those things too? Is there any way I could keep him? It's been so long since I've loved."

But God was silent. Yet even in His silence, I felt His answer. I also felt His sadness too, mirroring mine. What if I was not the right one for Jason? I needed to trust Jesus. But it was so hard!

"Okay," I sniffed. "I'll let him go. Please protect him. And please help me in the days to come." I ended my prayer and placed my forehead on the floor as I cried silently. *Okay, Maritza. You can do this.* This was on a Sunday in January of 2009. That Tuesday, I asked Jason to come over and I told him what needed to be said.

"What's wrong, baby?" he asked with that boyish grin on his face I'd come to love so much.

We were both seated on the couch in my living room. He had just come from the work site. He was happy to see me, but his smile faded when he saw my tears.

"You said something a few months back. You said you just knew we weren't going to last. I remember being sad and you said not to worry about it and that it was going to be okay. I think I understand now what you meant. I don't think we're going to work out. I'm so sorry, Jason."

He lowered his eyes and reality spread across his face. "Oh," he replied softly.

I placed my hand over his and squeezed tightly. Then I abruptly got up and ran to the bathroom. The emotions were so strong I thought I was going to throw up. Mary came home and began making small talk with Jason. I tried to compose myself in the bathroom. I felt sick to my stomach. The anxiety threatened to overtake me as it had in the past. I was afraid I would not be able to control my emotions or ever feel normal again. My heart was breaking. I was saying goodbye to the person I loved, and it was too much to bear. I couldn't breathe. I splashed some cool water on my face hoping to relieve the feverish feeling. After a few minutes, I walked back out into the living room and Jason was by the front door.

"Well, I guess I better head out," he said. I opened the door and he walked out and began walking up the steps but looked back and said, "It's gonna be okay, baby." Then he was gone, and I closed the door. Mary comforted me that night and for many nights after. The break-up threw me into a great depression that was stronger and longer than I care to admit.

Mami had always warned me to not put all my eggs into one basket. Unfortunately, that is exactly what I did. I put all my eggs, the bread, and the bacon into that basket! The thought hadn't occurred to me that we wouldn't last until the very end. As always, I decided to get my emotions out on paper:

> *Journal Entry: 10:52 am 1/17/2009*
> *Well, we broke up and I've been crying ever since. I keep thinking about going back to him but that would mean I'd have to give up on the idea of ever having a family with him. And I don't think he'd go to church with me, as I've always dreamed my future family would do. We've talked about it and he doesn't want me to give up what I want.*

But he said he couldn't see why we just couldn't have fun together and do the boyfriend/girlfriend thing. I want to do that, to just have fun and be with him. But if I went back to him, I'd take a chance on not knowing if he'd ever really fall in love with me. And I'd be with him knowing he couldn't give me what I need and deserve. Everything is telling me to move on—that I'd ruin everything for myself if I went back. I need to completely let go but it kills me. If I went back, would I be choosing Jason over God? I feel that God has saved me from being hurt even more if I stayed. I feel ungrateful and selfish in my sadness which makes it worse. Ariana asked how I was doing. I told her I was fine. She said that I am an influence on her. I must move on. I don't want Ariana to think this is how you act when things don't work out. I have to be careful in the decisions I make because someone is looking up to me. One day at a time. One step at a time. God is helping me through this. Don't abandon me, God. I know I'm being tested. I pray I pass. I love you so much.

I realized God didn't want me or Jason to give up on the things we both wanted out of life, but I just couldn't help my feelings from taking over again. I ended up missing work again because of anxiety and depression. I lost my appetite again and my weight plummeted. I lost about twenty-five pounds. I felt like there was nothing left to look forward to. Lying in bed at home, I would cry the day away.

When I did go to work, I would leave early because I just couldn't deal with it. My coworkers and others onsite began to take notice of my appearance and ask me if I was doing okay. I kept it all to myself, not wanting to tell anybody my business, of course. The only ones that knew were my sisters, Mami, and a few friends.

It was difficult seeing Jason at work every day and trying to focus on my tasks while at the same time ignoring the pain. It might have been easier if I never had to see him again. But that grace was not given to me. Writing was the only thing that helped get it out:

> *Journal Entry: 11:44 am 1/25/2009*
>
> *So, I'm going through the nervousness thing again. I try to eat and can't. My problem is, I don't look forward to much since Jason and I broke up. And I know it's wrong. It's been two weeks since our breakup. I can't allow this to get to me or hurt my job. I know I can't go back to him because it won't be the same. So why did I go through this? I can't ask that. I wanted a boyfriend and to love and that is what I got. But now I am by myself again. Now I understand why women go back to their men. Now I truly understand heartbreak. And I am tired of feeling sorry for myself. I guess I understand why some women stay in relationships that may not be good for them because they are afraid of what life would be like without them. But if we are so strong then why do we put ourselves through this? Even now, I want to call him because I believe I'll feel better when I do. But it's a false high, I guess. I miss him badly. But I know I have to keep going on and trust in my faith in God. I need to stop this heartbreak sickness. It's taken enough from me. Lord, help me through this. I know I'll make it through. It just seems hopeless now, that's all.*

Even though I knew deep down inside that Jason and I were not meant to be, the heart wants what the heart wants. The sadness of it all felt like the black hole had once again captured me. I was angry at times, and then felt an overwhelming sense of hopelessness and sadness at others. One morning on my way to work I prayed, as I usually do. It was the one time of day when I could get some quiet time with God.

"God, I know I keep praying for this. I know You are all powerful and can make it happen. If there is any way that Jason and I could be together again..."

"Stop," a voice commanded.

A firm yet gentle voice resonated inside of my mind. I didn't expect to actually hear God reply but every fiber in my body knew He was now communicating with me on this.

"He is not for you, little one," God replied. "I want you to stop praying for this. I have something better in store for you."

Wide-eyed and completely in shock, my hands tightened on the steering wheel and my back straightened up in my seat. An answer! Not the one I wanted at the time, but it was an answer! He had been listening to me! He also had been more than patient. I realized I was constantly praying this same prayer over and over.

After a few moments of dead silence, I responded. "Okay, Lord. I'll not pray this prayer anymore. Thank you, Lord. Thank you for answering me. Help me to come into agreement with Your Will in this." I prayed.

Despite the answer not being what my heart desired, and despite my sadness, I was strangely excited and happy that God had answered me in such a way that could not be denied. I began to feel a little hope.

Shortly after our breakup, Jason started dating another girl at the job site. She worked for the same company as he did. I saw them riding together from work one afternoon. They were ahead of me but as my pickup slowly passed them on the road leading out of the military complex, I looked over and saw him in the passenger seat. After that, I saw them together all the time on the job site. *So, this is her. She is his new girlfriend.* She was younger than me but I noticed right away we shared a lot in common in our appearance. This observation was interesting to me. We both had dark brown curly hair, were both petite and both of us had olive complexions. From the back, we must have appeared the same because one day on the job site a worker called me by her name.

Strangely enough, because of our similar appearance, I found it hard to be jealous or compare myself to her.

Yet, seeing them together every day made me wonder if I had done the right thing in letting Jason go. I wanted to be the one having fun and being with him and riding on the back of his motorcycle. He was easy to love and fun. But deep down I knew I wouldn't give up on the things I wanted out of life—a husband who shared my faith and children to love. Having an answer from God eased the pain of knowing Jason and I would never be together again. I felt that God was with me, that He was close. Feeling His presence, I knew He was helping me get through the breakup and, in time, I would be okay.

Chapter Eighteen
Relief and Restoration

I don't know why I went through that struggle. Why does anybody have to struggle? I do know it made me stronger. I continued going to church and joined the Spanish Choir. Singing old Spanish hymns reminded me of when I sang with Abuelita in her church choir when I was a young girl visiting her back in the Bronx.

We'd walk through the courtyard and the park behind her building together. She'd talk about the love of Jesus and how His mother, Mary, would pray for us to stay close to her Son. Singing those same songs as an adult brought those happy memories back.

Through those memories, I felt God holding me in His Arms. He was reminding me of another form of true love, the kind that heals. Once again, God brought me out of that pit of hopeless heartbreak just like He had done many times before. He reminded me through my love of singing how strong I was and where I came from. When I'd look into Abuelita's eyes, I saw pure love and strength there.

"Remember that, little one," He said. I was more than a conqueror and I had that same strength. I was a masterpiece and deeply loved. If I ever doubted that, I needed only to open my

Bible to remind myself what God thought of me. I began to feel better and better with each passing day.

As I continued to recover from the depression, my job performance steadily improved. Doing all of the normal tasks of running a satellite office, performing inspections, and managing my team, my confidence flowed back into me. My swag had finally returned and I remembered who I was—a hard worker who is compassionate and caring but above all, a child of Almighty God.

My company had secured two more jobs with another JV contractor, who had in turn chosen me to lead inspections for those projects. They were impressed with my work ethic, proprietary interest, and sheer passion for getting the job done. This JV contractor wanted me and only me for each of the jobs that I secured for my company. I had been on the project at the military installation for two years. At the end of my time there I began to reminisce about the past years. Sitting in my work pick-up, in the newly constructed parking lot, I recalled when the area was a large field and a few brown military-style buildings sat on it. I remember meeting Mark back when we took our geography class together. Our class was in one of those brown buildings that once stood where I now sat in my truck.

It's funny how life brought me back to this same spot many years later to inspect its reconstruction. It had gone from a few brown buildings and a field to a campus of multiple sprawling buildings, roads, parking lots, and underground utilities. Now many people would occupy these buildings and perform research and testing for the U.S. Military and our country, bringing it further into the 21st century with new technology and ideas. I got to be a part of this land's makeover and the future of my country moving forward. That felt good!

❊

The second job that I secured was for the Flight 93 Memorial Park in Shanksville, PA, a town that would change my life beyond what I could have ever imagined and not far from where my samples came from during my final research project in college. It was in Shanksville where I would finally be released from the sorrow of my last breakup and where God would show me how happy I could be.

The future park is about three hours from my home so there had to be another option than driving to and from work. One morning my boss and I rode together to the site to attend a meeting about the job. It was my first time going there. I saw the landscape change the further west we drove. Mountains began to appear like gentle waves, rising and falling for miles. I saw countless farms and homes sprinkled among them. I observed many animals and was surprised to see sheep! I couldn't remember the last time I had seen a farm that had sheep. I noticed the quietness and how it became breezier the further we drove up the mountains.

There weren't many stores that I recognized, and certainly no cities. At least, not the kind I was used to. I saw "ma and pa" shops, farm stores, and a gun shop. We passed a garden shop with the most beautiful large flowering baskets I'd ever seen. I told myself when I came up, I was going to stop there and get one. The rolling green hills and mountains continued. As a Geology major, I was excited to see folding in the rock outcrops on the side of the roads.

A rock outcrop is a rock formation that is visible on the surface. Folding is the bending of rock occurring over millions of years. Outcrops are sometimes seen along highways. The last part of the ride took us straight up another mountain and when we reached the top there was a lookout point with a sign that read Maryland, Pennsylvania, and West Virginia. From those 2900 feet in elevation, you could see all three states.

We arrived at an old concrete building with a rusted tin roof where the meeting was held. I looked over the plans for the park as the contractor went over the details with my boss. I was getting excited. After the meeting, the superintendent for the contractor company, Gary, took us out to the edge of the lot where the old building stood, and it was there that we could see the whole park. He explained that the area was once a coal mine that was closed down and the old building was the office for that operation many years ago. Then he pointed out into the field to a large stone that sat by itself. He told us that was where the nose of the plane hit on September 11, 2001. It is believed that the plane was headed to the Capitol in Washington, DC. He told us the story of the passengers that took back the plane and sacrificed themselves to save our nation's capital.

There was a sobering feeling about the place. I looked out along the vast quiet landscape of rolling green and rocky hills and wondered what it would say if it could speak.

After the meeting, my boss wanted to meet with someone about a house she was looking to rent for me. I would live in Pennsylvania for the week while I inspected the work at the park and return home to Maryland on the weekends. I was a little nervous about being so far away from home and not knowing anyone but Gary, who made me feel secure. We worked together at the military installation, it was nice knowing someone in this new place.

We drove up to a beautiful white farmhouse with a red roof and a big red barn. The house was situated in the middle of a vast field and stuck out like a shining jewel. It looked like something out of Country Home magazine. We drove up the long driveway, parked, and walked up to the front porch. That's when I met Laura Miller. Her welcoming smile instantly put me at ease. She ran a bed and breakfast out of her home and offered me a room.

The job started with a lot of mass movement of earth for the new road that was going in. Every day after work, I was invited to have dinner with the Miller family. I was quickly growing to love them and their hospitality. They had five grandchildren, four boys, and one girl, whom I lovingly call "my princess." I fell in love with all of them. They took me fishing at a pond they had on their land and four-wheeling which I had never done before. We went swimming in the lake when it got hot, and I even had my first shooting experience at a target practice area in the woods. Laura told me the story of when the plane crashed on 9/11 and how the town came together to help tell the story of the passengers. She also shared that the plane crashed not far from their land and that from their pond you could see the large stone. Every day, a volunteer from Shanksville, including Laura, her husband Roger, and his parents, whom I lovingly called "Grandma and Grandpa," would take time out of their day and go to the temporary memorial on the site and tell visitors all about Flight 93.

They were called Ambassadors. Other residents from Shanksville and the neighboring towns volunteered as well. Laura would also tell me about the history of their town and about the mining incident at Que Creek, where nine miners who made national headlines were rescued in July of 2002. Her husband Roger, who owned an engineering firm, helped locate the miners by using surveying equipment that was able to tell the drillers where to drill the shaft to bring up the miners.

I told Laura that God had truly blessed their family. Laura and I spent many hours together, even on some weekends when I decided to stay because I was having so much fun. I helped weed and plant flowers with her, learned to feed the animals on their farm, and collect eggs from their chicken coop. The steer and the horses were kept in the larger barn. In that year and a half, I met so many wonderful people including more of Laura and Roger's family, whom I adopted as my own. I experienced so many wonderful things that I felt my depression release its grip on me. I had fallen in love with the Millers and their five, funny, non-stop-action, fun-loving grandkids. Because Laura and I were so close, her grandkids became my grandkids!

I was there when their goats had babies, and even helped in naming one of them "Lucky." My princess and I named her that because her birth was not an easy one. She was a scrawny white goat with brown ears, one of which was folded over itself. When she was born, she plopped out onto the ground and didn't move at first. She had difficulty getting up and sadly, her mother didn't pay much attention to her. Mama goat moved on to the other newborn that was having more success moving around and Lucky was left to fend for herself. I wasn't leaving her though; my princess and I were going to stay with her until we knew Lucky was safe. We kept encouraging her to get up. She started to move her head a little and began to raise herself from the ground. She plopped back down again and again due to the slipperiness of the afterbirth, but she didn't give up. She was a fighter! Finally, she was on her feet, and my princess and I cheered. She was indeed lucky to be alive.

Lucky quickly thrived under our care. For some reason, the mother would not let Lucky suck from her teat, so we had to make milk bottles and feed her. I learned to mix the goat milk powder with warm water and put it in a large bottle with a rubber nipple to feed Lucky. Every day at feeding time when I rolled up in my pick-up, Lucky would get excited and get through the fence and run up to me. She was so little the fence couldn't hold her. This little baby depended on me and seeing that innocent dependence filled me with such warmth and purpose. It got me thinking, how could I possibly have time to be depressed when I was busy feeding and mothering an adorable baby goat who needed me?

I helped plant the Millers' garden and can the vegetables they grew. I helped tie ribbons for the party favors for Laura's son's wedding, which I attended, feeling just like one of the family. Attending sports games for the grandkids, eating country home cooking, riding four-wheelers, shooting guns, boating, swimming, and enjoying God's creation gave me such a constant high, I never wanted to come down. I think I even became a Steelers fan (but don't tell anybody). Laura let me get on her zero-turn John Deer mower once. I got a little scared so I left that one to the grandkids to maneuver! We went to church, cooked church dinners, and I enjoyed my first apple dumpling! I think country living agreed with me.

One day at the site, Gary advised me to go sit and hear the whole story about Flight 93 at the temporary memorial from one of the Ambassadors. At lunch, I took his advice. I walked along the makeshift wall adorned with gifts, tokens, and trinkets from visitors who left them in gratitude for the passengers of Flight 93. Afterward, I made it over to one of the benches and sat down and listened to the whole story. As I did, I began to understand what happened and truly mourn those that lost their lives that day. I realized they were more than just passengers; they were people with families and stories of their own. It was then that the importance of that place would cement itself into my heart forever.

I was becoming a part of something much bigger than myself. No one can undo the past or bring anyone back, but we can turn the ugly thing that happened around and tell the story so that no one would forget what these brave people did for us. This park was going to be a healing place for our nation and a reminder that we stood united, and would never forget. A whole new respect grew inside of me, and I told myself I was going to do the best job I could at the park to help convey the story and honor the fallen.

During my time off from the job site, I would visit the neighboring towns, circling them on my map in a magazine Laura gave me about the county they lived in. One of the areas I visited was Que Creek. I saw the shaft that the miners were brought up in. It was left as part of the monument. Driving around the county, I was in awe and grateful for its beauty. My favorite season was fall because of all the colors. I drove up onto a high point on the job site, parked, and took in the incredible view. The reds, purples, browns, oranges, and yellows of fall took my breath away. I kept trying to take photos but could never truly capture the landscape's beauty. It was as if God was telling me, no, little one, no photo could ever replicate what I have created for you. I want you to enjoy these live. So, I did!

In a short time, I had become a country girl and I was loving every minute of it. I loved the mud between my toes, the grass beneath my feet, and the water down my back, and I thanked God every day because I was so happy. After the loss of my last relationship, I felt the sun come up again.

Chapter Nineteen
Hellos and Goodbyes

As the Flight 93 project was coming to a close, I began to worry about having to leave my farm family for good. I dreaded the sorrow I knew I'd feel leaving this place that had broadened my horizon and saved me from myself. The thought of leaving increased my anxiety. My worrying caused more worrying and ultimately, I worried that I would return to my old, depressed self. My time in Shanksville had created such wonderful memories that the thought of leaving started to fill me with despair. I was afraid that once I left the Millers, my life would go back to the way it was before—boring, non-active, and depressive.

I knew that when I was home in Maryland, it was different. Mary and I lived together but we were far from the rest of our family. Papi was less than ten miles down the road, but he had his issues he was dealing with, and at times they would trigger anxiety in me.

Being around such a big family in Shanksville, there was always something going on. This wasn't the case at home. That's when the thoughts would start—at home while I was idle. In Shanksville, my thoughts didn't have a chance to burden me. Life there was full and active and colorful. I allowed myself to think that happiness is only present in certain locations. But that is not true—you take happiness with you, the same way you take anything else with you. I realized I had made the mistake of allowing my new Pennsylvania family to be my salvation from depression to the point it made me sick to leave them. What was next? I worried.

One morning at breakfast I had some sausage and pancakes. The sausage seemed a bit greasy and the pancakes old, but I ate them just the same and then left for work. I arrived at the field office and loaded my John Deere gator as usual and drove out to the job site. A few hours passed and I started to get nauseous. *I hope I don't throw up; I hate throwing up!* Well, that's all it took. All of a sudden, my thoughts started to spiral and a cool feeling began to race down my arms. Adrenaline. *Here we go.* Nervousness began which irritated my stomach more than it already was and since I was already sensitive to the fact that my time with the Millers was coming to an end, it didn't take long for the anxiety to course through me like a raging river. I leaned out of my gator and vomited in the dirt. I just let it go, not caring that the crew could see me as they drove by in their large construction dump trucks. When I finished, I wiped my mouth, turned the key in the ignition, and began to race back to the field office, hoping the cool breeze on my damp face would calm me back down. It didn't.

The mounting attack rose inside the way a rogue wave suddenly appears in the middle of the ocean, out of nowhere. I feared it would wash over me and drown me in complete fear. The wave had been building and building for weeks, there was no way I could outrun the tsunami rushing toward and inside of me. "No, please...no." I said in heavy breaths as the wave finally overtook me.

"It's here! Oh God, it's here!" I said aloud. I raced down the old road toward the steel building in my John Deere gator, pedal to the metal. I knew no matter how fast I drove; I would not escape it. I never could. "Let me get there, please! Just let me get there!"

I finally reached the construction office and pulling into the garage, I shouted to my contractor, "Gary! Gary!"

He rushed out of the office and seeing the pitiful state I was in, took action. I don't even remember what he said when he reached me. All I could tell him to do was one thing: "Hold me!" And he did.

The panic attack had arrived in full force, and I knew I needed an anchor. He locked one hand onto my left shoulder and held me firm as the attack racked my body. I began to vomit uncontrollably. I could no longer process my senses—hearing, smell, and taste were muted, gone. But sight and touch were intensified. All I could do was vomit liquid onto the floor of my gator. My body flapped like a rag doll from the convulsions. I could not stop it or control it. His firm grip on me held me sure because there was no way I could get through this on my own strength. Adrenalin coursed through my veins like molten lava. My skin was ultra-sensitized so that the light wind on that Pennsylvania mountaintop felt like a thousand needles sticking me at once.

My mind was a blur. All I could do was focus on the floor of my gator where my insides surrendered all that was in me, waiting for the attack to end. Finally, it released some of its hold on me and I was spent. Gary helped me out of the gator and into a chair in his office where I let my body slump and my arms fall to my sides. Fitz, the quality control manager for the construction of the park, was also present and began to clean my gator with a hose outside. I had no strength left and felt like rubber. Then the urge came to go to the bathroom and finish from the other end. I didn't think I could do it. I felt that I would go right there and then, and the fear came again. Yet somehow, I mustered up whatever strength I had left and made it to the toilet.

Afterward, completely drained, I slowly returned to the chair. I asked Gary to call Laura to take me home to the farm. The attack was over for now and I needed to return to my comfort zone and recharge. Sitting in that chair, one question loomed in my mind. Would I turn left and allow this attack to sink me into depression again...or would I turn right for a change?

Laura came and took me home and I got some rest. The morning after, as I lay in bed, I waited for the familiar morning nervousness that always follows after such an attack but it never came. I waited for the depression to take root but it didn't. I decided to get up and go to work as normal, refusing to call out and stay in bed as I'd done in years passed. *No more pity party here. I can do this; I can go to work.* As I sat in my truck on the site, I felt a calmness in me. Strange. But after years of the opposite, I'll take it!

One day while at the farm, I was watching TV in the living room and a commercial came on advertising a program called Attacking Anxiety and Depression. Well, this is nice! I thought. Right on time! Anticipating the return of my panic attacks, I decided to take that "right" turn and order the program.

The program came with CDs on how and why panic attacks begin, how to control your thinking, how to become more assertive, learning to relax and a life coach to help you through. The founder, Lucinda Bassett, spoke with others in group form and enlisted the help of a psychiatrist who would speak about the science part of depression and anxiety. I listened intently to the CDs on my way to and from work. It was easy to just pop the next CD in and listen as I drove. The people in the group shared their intimate stories about their struggles with depression, anxiety, and panic. I came to see that their battles mirrored my own. Listening to their stories helped me better understand my anxiety and that I should not give myself such a hard time for being human. I learned that people who struggle with anxiety can be incredibly sensitive. I have always been very sensitive to others' feelings as well as my own.

I also learned that anxious and depressive people tend to be overly concerned with their emotions. This rang true for me because I was always over-analyzing everything I felt. The program also revealed to me that because I had spent so much time thinking negatively about myself and my situation, of course, I always felt bad.

If I was going to be free from this cycle, I had to learn how to replace my negative thoughts with positive ones. The program helped me understand that it took time for my negative thinking to become a bad habit, and bad habits take time to break. Some people break their habits after a few months. Some take longer, but the point is that they break their habit by continuing to follow the steps that are in line with their goals.

Part of the struggle with depression and anxiety is that relaxing is almost impossible to do. Jason used to tell me to relax all the time. I thought there was no one more relaxed than me—I loved to sleep! But I was beginning to see that relaxation was about more than just sleep.

One morning while in bed, I decided to try replacing my first thoughts with positive ones. *Okay, let's try this thing. I want to stay in bed but….no don't start with a negative thought. Today is going to be okay. I will get through it. It's okay to feel yucky.* I waited to 'pop above the line' as I once heard when dealing with emotions. I lay there waiting to feel different, motivated. "Well, that didn't work too well," I sighed. "I guess I have to keep trying—every day."

To keep myself from going nuts, I always had to keep moving, working, or doing something that kept my mind concentrating on anything other than my depression. That is why being in Shanksville was so good for me—there was never a dull moment!

Idle time was bad for me because thoughts would start running through my head, and I'd get anxious. Have you ever heard the old saying, "an idle mind is the devil's workshop?" Well, in my experience, it's very true. I used to spend time catastrophizing about anything and everything. I would talk myself out of doing things that usually would appeal to me because of fear.

Once I wanted to visit my college buddy Kaitlyn's parents, but I didn't go because I feared getting sick with anxiety on the long drive. I imagined getting stranded with a flat tire an hour away from home. I'd usually forego the pleasure of doing something enjoyable because I felt anxious about something terrible that could happen along the way. I'd tell myself; I'll do it later or I'll visit them when I feel better, making excuses.

Anxiety was always there like a pest that just wouldn't go away. It didn't go away because I still dealt with the fear of the physical symptoms of the panic attack that would soon follow. I started asking myself, What's the worst that can happen to me if I have a panic attack? I anticipated feeling miserable during the attacks, but I knew that eventually, they would subside. I dreaded the feeling of being drained of energy from the attacks, but I knew there was always some energy left in me. I began practicing positive self-talk, replacing scary thoughts with upbeat ones, but it took a while to get the hang of it.

One of my tasks while working at the memorial park was taking concrete cylinders that I molded onsite to a laboratory in Johnstown, about forty minutes from where I was staying at the farm. The lab broke the concrete cylinders for me and reported their strengths in PSI (pounds per square inch). This had to be done and because of the amount of concrete at the site, delivering the cylinders was a weekly trip. In the beginning, I was fine taking them there but as my time was coming to a close in this haven of mine, it became a weekly struggle due to my ever-increasing anxiety. I tried the thought replacement again:

Journal Entry: 2010

Am I going to have to force myself to eat because I'm nervous? No. You will eat as you always do. It will be okay. Having a bad time controlling my thoughts. It's okay, this is a bad habit that you are breaking.

I fear having a panic attack on my way to Johnstown. It'll be okay. I can do it.

What happens if my anxiety comes back? What happens if I have a hard time going to Johnstown? If it comes back, try not to worry about it. It will go away. Don't think too much about going to Johnstown. You will be fine like you always are when you go. It's going to be okay.

Sitting in my white pickup, hands on the wheel, I breathed deeply. As each 'what if' barged into my mind, I practiced allowing it to float out without emotionally responding. It wasn't easy at first, but I was determined to keep going.

Every time a bad or fearful thought crept in, threatening to ruin my day, I'd call it by an ugly name and tell it to be quiet and sit down. This brought a little laughter inside of me which diffused how serious I was making the situation out to be. If you can laugh at something or even yourself, it takes the pressure off.

Listening to sermons and encouraging talks on Christian radio, and pastors such as Joel Osteen, brought more hope to my life. I heard Joel Osteen say having faith in God is trusting Him when life doesn't make sense. Every time a phrase or Scripture verse struck me, I would write it down on post-it notes and put them wherever I could see them---my dashboard, my checkbook, a lamp shade, etc. Living with anxiety and depression can make life seem impossible. Having support and a community around you that doesn't judge you, but lifts you up in your struggles, can make the struggle easier to get through. Support is very important in this way. Even though I didn't share what I was feeling with most of my friends in Shanksville, people were praying for me, nonetheless.

One morning while driving to the memorial park site, I was listening to the local Christian radio station, K-Love. They were asking for donations to continue bringing God's message over the airways. I loved hearing the inspirational music, so I decided to give. As soon as I parked my work truck, I dialed the number given on the radio. A few days later back at home in Maryland for the weekend, I received a call from an unknown number.

I answered my cell and a nice lady whose name I cannot recall warmly greeted me.

"Hi, may I speak to Maritza?" the lady asked.

Groggy from sleeping on the couch (in an attempt to escape the depression), I answered, "This is she."

"I'm calling from K-Love. I wanted to thank you for your donation to the station and ask, how can I pray for you?"

Oh, man did this come out of nowhere! I wasn't even expecting to ever hear back from the station and had forgotten all about the donation. Lying on my couch in the dark living room, blinds closed, keeping the world away, I teared up as I told her how.

"I've been dealing with depression, and I want to be healed from it. I'm sad all the time and I don't want to do anything. I don't know what to do anymore, I feel so hopeless."

The tears were dropping hot and heavy now. It seemed so easy to unburden myself with someone I didn't know.

"Maritza, I just want you to know that everyone here will be praying for you and over you. You don't have to go through this alone," she said gently and with understanding. And she prayed for me. A total stranger prayed for me. A call came through my darkness and shone a light. I could have let it go to voicemail as I do with all strange numbers, but I didn't. The Lord arrived as He always did, letting me know I was not forgotten, and instead that I was seen and loved.

I decided to spend that Fourth of July holiday at the farm, especially since I would be leaving for good in a few days. I wanted to make the most of my time there, spending it with the family I'd grown to love so much. On the evening of the Fourth, as the sun was setting, a bunch of us crowded onto Grandpa Miller's pontoon boat and headed out on the lake to see the fireworks.

It was a perfect night. The air was cool and crisp, the sky was the deepest darkest blue I'd ever seen, and the flicker of stars began to shine through. I loved being out on the boat on the lake. It was so relaxing riding over the gentle waves and being with those I loved. As the moon ascended into the night sky, the first of many spectacular fireworks shot up and pierced the dark sky. Will it ever be like this after I leave? Could life get any more perfect? I thought about all of this and felt a sting of pain in my heart. That night, as always, I took to writing:

> *Journal Entry: 10:11 pm 7/4/2011*
> *I've been depressed with the thought of saying goodbye to the Millers. I've gotten so close to them. I've been crying on and off for the past two hours. I talked to Mami about it, and it was killing me not to talk to Laura. So, I finally did a little and she knew. She was washing her van. I thought, maybe she keeps herself busy so she doesn't dwell on the sad stuff. I can learn that from her. But I will miss her most of all. We had a nice weekend at the lake for the Fourth of July. We all got on Grandpa Miller's boat to see the fireworks. The boat ended up dying so Laura's son and his wife had to tow us back. That is a memory none*

of us will forget. I hope that I don't wake up with too much anxiety. But if I do, I pray I will deal with it. I feel better now. Off to bed. I am ready for this new chapter of my life to begin.

Finally, it was my last night with the Millers and Laura had made a wonderful spread for me. I was feeling so many emotions---sadness at leaving, happiness at seeing all who came over to say goodbye, and anxiety about the future. What was so special about the evening was that although it would be our last night with me living there, I was reminded of how much I was loved and how much love I had for them. We had a great time eating and talking about memories we shared.

After everyone had left for home, I sat on my bed in the room that had become mine while living at the farm and wrote:

> *Journal Entry: 10:32 pm 7/6/11*
> *Well, tonight's my last night. Laura cooked steak and shrimp for me, my last dinner, and all the grandkids and her kids came. Sonia (Roger's sister) and Grandma Miller came too. I am sad to leave but I think I'm all cried out. Mami and Paul will be here tomorrow to help me drive home. Paul is such a great friend. Laura told me she likes him. I had terrible anxiety today, but I got through it. I listened to Laura talk about all the places she's traveled to with Roger and all I can think about is how I'd have anxiety. It's always in my brain. Will it ever set me free? I hope so. I must believe that everything will be okay. Thank God for His love. I know I'll be fine.*

The next morning, I went outside to play with Laura's youngest grandson, John. John was a cutie pie, with white-blonde hair, fair, and full of energy as most two-year-olds usually are. John loved it when I pushed him on the swing out by the barn. As we began our normal routine of me pushing him and him laughing at the playful noises I made, he asked:

"Rissa, you going away?"

"Yes, John. I'm leaving soon."

"But where you going?" he innocently asked.

"I'm going back home."

"But your home is there!" and he pointed to the farmhouse.

I teared up. I knew it was true. Being there had been my home and always would be.

"Yes, but I mean my Maryland home. I will be back again to play with you soon," I promised, trying to keep the tears from falling.

Soon, Paul drove up with Mami and it was time to leave. Mami got to meet the Millers for the first time. She was very grateful to them for all they had done for me. After some light conversation between her and Roger about the farm and garden, it was time to say our goodbyes. Laura hugged me tightly, tears forming in her eyes.

"You take care now. We'll see each other again," she smiled through her tears.

My tears were all dried up but the sadness remained just the same.

"Thank you for everything. Love you." And with that, I got into my work truck with Mami in the passenger seat and Paul following in his car. As I drove away, I thought how different it would be not returning here next week as I had done for so many weeks before. I was glad Paul brought Mami up here to drive down with me because, in my saddened state, I wasn't sure if I was going to be hit with a panic attack and need her to drive. That was the reason they had come. I wasn't sure I could trust myself leaving on my own without breaking down in tears. Driving down the mountain, I felt a little stronger with Mami by my side. Once again, I needed to rely on her strength and once again she was there to provide it.

Chapter Twenty
Sliding Backwards

When I think back to all the times I've relapsed, I remember Mami was always right by my side. I knew she couldn't understand what I was going through at first because I could barely explain it myself, but she always had a word or deed of encouragement for me. Even when she was promoted to a managerial position and moved to Virginia, she would still make sure to tell me how much she loved me. I knew she needed me around too, which was important for me. One of the ways I used to eliminate my negative thoughts was to remind myself that I am loved and needed here in this world.

Mami, my sisters, and I started a new tradition in 2005, after my college graduation. We began taking "girls' trips" together every year. We've been to the Grand Canyon and Las Vegas, on two cruises to the Caribbean and Mexico, Montreal and Quebec City, Canada, Puerto Rico, Hawaii, and Bethany Beach, Delaware. On one of those trips, we were supposed to go to Venice, Italy to visit Joshua who was stationed there while in the military. We were so excited to go back to Europe. We booked our trip in December of 2010, yet soon realized that was not a great decision—a severe snowstorm was immobilizing parts of Europe and our flight to

Italy was canceled. I was on the phone with the airlines trying to figure out a way to get there.

"Your connecting flight into Paris is canceled due to the snowstorm. We don't have any other connections for you at this time until the storm lets up," the airline official said.

"Do you know when that will be or when another airport will open up?" I asked feeling my hope slip away.

"No. We do not know when the storm will let up. Since the tickets are non-refundable, we can book you for another trip later or you can choose now if you would like to go somewhere else."

Somewhere else? I thought.

"Um, okay hold on a minute." I turned to Mami and the girls.

"Guys, they can't connect us to Italy because of the storm. Seems it's worse than we thought. But she is asking if we want to go anywhere else."

"Anywhere?" Mami chimed in, her eyebrows raised. "Mira, vamos pa' Puerto Rico!"

"Yeah, let's go to Puerto Rico!" joined the girls.

I turned back to the phone, "Um, miss, are you still there?"

"Yes ma'am, I am here. Do you have a decision?"

"Yes. We would like to switch our destination to Puerto Rico please."

The receptionist confirmed the new reservation and told us when to get to the airport the next day. By seven the following morning, we found ourselves on a flight to San Juan, Puerto Rico. Instead of spending Christmas in an ancient city in Europe, we were spending it in the tropics with no snow in the forecast!

I remember arriving in Puerto Rico and thinking, okay, I got on the plane and did fine. Now it's time to have fun. We arrived at my Uncle Pedro's house in the mountains. Coincidentally, Ezra was already there on vacation. Tio (Spanish for "uncle") Pedro came to pick us up at the airport and we were all happy to see each other.

When we pulled up to the house, my aunt came out with a sign that said, "Welcome to Italy." We laughed and hugged her and Ezra. We didn't get to spend the holidays with Joshua but we did get to spend them with Ezra and the rest of our family in Puerto Rico. It was bittersweet for me since the last time I had been to Puerto Rico I was sixteen. Now, at thirty, I was able to see how my family had grown over the years and I had a new appreciation for them.

Tio Pedro and my aunt cooked us up a nice meal of meat and potato salad and we enjoyed each other, eating and catching up. Afterward, Tio Pedro took us up on his roof to show us the view of the City of Caguas below. Even when I visit now, it is still one of the most beautiful views I've ever seen. Nestled in the valley between a vast mountain range is the city below with the sea in the distance. At night, all the lights are lit, and it looks like stars sitting on the earthen floor. I never get tired of that view.

A few days into our trip, we visited my grandparents in a neighboring town. Most of my aunts and uncles were there and everyone was celebrating and eating. I began to catch up with another uncle, Tio Manuel, who writes and sings Christian music for his church in Puerto Rico. Tio Manuel is a fun-loving, comical, jovial person. You will always catch him with a smile. He told me about how his work had taken him to Miami and about the famous people he has met. He was interested in my musical ability and showed a genuine desire in helping me. I began to talk to him about my desire to sing.

"Tell me, sobrina. What types of genres do you like to sing? You also write songs, yes?"

"Si Tio! I love all types of musical genres, especially our native cultural music. I've been writing songs since I was a young teenager, but I don't think they are any good."

"Ah! Don't say that. I'm sure your songs are very good and it makes me happy you write and sing. I will help you in whatever way you need. I have confidence in you. I am here to help you and I would love to."

"Really? Oh, Tio, I am so excited! Thank you!"

"Let's stay in touch and I can send you some beats that you can sing to, and then you can record and send them back to me. What do you say?"

I was over the moon. I have such a musical family, yet it never dawned on me to ask them for their guidance. And my Tio Manuel was offering it to me so generously. "I say yes Tio!"

My grandmother was pouring soda into cups for the family, and I grabbed one. As soon as I drank some of it, the familiar panicky feelings started bubbling up. With the mounting feelings building, I had the urge to go to the bathroom, so I excused myself and hurried downstairs.

Once in the bathroom, I started shaking and feeling light-headed. Of course, being concerned with the way I felt all the time worried me and, this intensified the panic attack. I called for Mary and told her to tell Mami I was not feeling well and that we needed to leave. I left without saying goodbye to my grandparents and the rest of my family. I felt ungrateful that I rushed out of there, not wanting to give a reason for my quick departure.

Once in the car, I reclined the seat and closed my eyes. I didn't want to see anything. I only wanted to get back to Tio Pedro's house and relax. Here we go again, just when I thought I could let my hair down. Anxiety and panic attacks always ruin my good times and I end up submitting to them. All I can do when it hits me is to find a safe place away from people, a comfort zone so that I can concentrate on feeling better.

My aunt and Mami and my sisters got into the car, and we drove back to Tio Pedro's house, which I had designated my comfort zone. I went upstairs, changed my clothes, took a Xanax, and welcomed the oblivion of sleep that occurs after such an attack. Because of the strength God had given me, and the help that the books and programs had brought me, I didn't wake up the next morning feeling worse and I didn't fall into a deep depression. Instead, I allowed myself an easy, relaxing day at the house.

I had another attack a few days later when my cousins, my sisters, and I took a drive to a beach on the other side of the island. Driving there, I kept thinking I hope the panic attack doesn't come back.

But because I was anticipating it, I suffered another. Still, we walked to the beach and put our feet into the water, and took pictures. I felt maybe I was okay because I love the beach. But once everyone started to get hungry and decided to buy lunch, the thoughts began to surge again: What if I can't eat like before? What if I have diarrhea and can't make it back to the house? We're over an hour away. What if these panic attacks ruin my vacation? What if, what if, what if...

In the past, when one panic attack would happen, I'd be in constant fear of another. It would take over my mind to the point of overwhelming me and more attacks eventually followed. The uncomfortable feelings that occurred in my grandparent's house began a cycle of anticipation which led to more attacks.

My cousins wanted to take my sisters and me to a tropical rainforest in Puerto Rico called El Yunque. We drove to the rainforest, stopping at one of the waterfalls. If I wasn't in panic mode, I would have been able to enjoy the beauty of the falls. Instead, as I got out of the car and forced myself to walk toward them, the world started to get fuzzy. My head felt like it would lift off my shoulders. I could see my sisters and cousins having fun at the falls and taking photos, but I felt as if I were in another dimension—not in the same realm as everyone else. Due to this uneasy feeling, my worrying increased, and I finally had to tell my cousin to take us back to the house because I wasn't feeling well.

Though disappointed with the disruption to their day, my sisters felt bad for me, which made me feel bad as well, but I didn't know what else to do so I took a Xanax. I knew myself well enough to realize that I needed to get to my safe place to relax my way through these attacks.

Despite all that, I was able to enjoy most of the rest of the trip until it was time to leave. I started to worry about getting on the plane to return home. I had been okay during the arrival flight because it had been a long time since I had experienced an attack. Having had multiple attacks while in Puerto Rico, I was now unsettled about the flight and the potential for turbulence, which scared me to death.

I kept thinking about my house and my cats and how I wanted to be home, but I could only get there if I got on the plane. I was nervous at the airport but figured if I'd come this far then I could go further. We boarded the flight, and I sat in the middle next to Mary. As soon as we were up in the air, I put the tray down from the seat in front of me and laid my head on it to try to get some sleep. I could never sleep on a plane, but I wanted to close my eyes and block out my surroundings. If I didn't see it, maybe I could forget where I was. During the flight home, I did experience a few minor panic attacks, but with nowhere to go, I decided to just breathe slowly, a technique I hadn't used in the past. As I breathed in and out in a slow, rhythmic pattern, my uneasiness vanished, and the adrenaline subsided. I realized I had just learned a new way to get through them. Just breathe, Maritza. Breathe.

Chapter Twenty-One

And Forward Again

Using the aids I had obtained; my CD program, books, my medicine, and the biggest tool of all, my faith, I began to feel much better about my condition. I tried to give my worries to God, but it was difficult because I worried for so long. I am learning every day that things always seem to work out for the best somehow. Knowing that God is watching over me gives me greater peace than anything else.

Although I cannot get those missed moments back, I learned to acknowledge and appreciate myself for engaging in the ones I didn't miss. I decided once more to live in the present, to leave the past behind, and to trust the future with God. Feeling guilty for past mistakes only leads to more guilt and shame and I was so fed up with living that way.

I began taking a tally of the guilty and regretful thoughts I placed on myself and the incredible amount of pressure that came with them. I started with thoughts about my childhood dream of becoming a singer. I felt that when I didn't sing well, I was nothing special. But I reminded myself that this dream wasn't by mistake. I didn't put it there—God did, and that meant it was real and important. God loves me even if I struggle to love myself. He made me who I am so that must be good, right? My identity is not tied to my musical dream. My identity is in Jesus Christ, and I am a child of the Most High. I am so much more than my ability to sing. If ever I doubt that again I just need to read His Word to see that I am "fearfully and wonderfully made." I am His child first and everything else is just details, enhancements to what is already there. The same for every living soul on earth.

The Attacking Anxiety and Depression program explained that people living with guilt tend to live in the past while those with anxiety or who struggle with panic attacks tend to live in the future. This resonated with me because all of my panic attacks occurred with me thinking, what if this happens? What if that happens? Then guilt and depression would come when I thought, what could have happened … or what should I have done differently? I was totally exhausted. Staying in the present can be difficult for people with anxiety and depression, but I was determined that it was not impossible.

Months later, I was invited to attend the wedding of an old high school friend which was going to be held in Kansas City. I had sent my RSVP confirming that I would be going—or would I?

My good friend Paul offered to accompany me to help me through my fears. We had traveled together to Europe back in 2009 and I remember having a blast. If Paul goes with me, it won't be so bad. We've always traveled well together. I started to feel a little more secure.

Paul asked me to ask my friend if he could be my "plus one" at the wedding because he knew I wanted to go. "Why don't you ask your friend if it's okay that I go with you? That way you are not alone and I can be there for you. You know we'll have fun!"

"That's a great idea. Okay, I'll ask her tonight." That evening, I phoned my friend nervously and asked her if I could bring a guest.

I thought, who does that? Asking to bring someone to a wedding who is not invited? I mean, you gotta pay per plate, she doesn't even know Paul... I must be out of my mind. However, once she realized how having a great friend like Paul by my side would help with the traveling, she graciously agreed and expressed that she really wanted me there. It was all coming together. Part of me wished it hadn't. Anxious and fearful, I would have loved an excuse to get out of getting on another plane. However, I knew that the guilt and depression of missing such an event would have been worse. Deep down I really wanted to go.

I procrastinated with booking the trip even though Paul would remind me occasionally. It took him coming over to my office at work for me to finally book the airline tickets.

"Maritza, you are going to this wedding! Paul said. You know how important it is."

"Okay, okay," I said hastily, as I pulled up the travel page on the internet.

"Here. Take my credit card. Book it. My treat," he said, generously. This was happening way too easily. I felt that everything was indeed lining up for us to go. I started to believe God wanted this for me. I only needed to trust Him. After I booked the reservation and received the confirmation on the trip, I felt a little cold shiver go down my spine. "It's booked."

"Okay great. Now let's go get something to eat!"

As the days got closer to our departure date, I kept thinking about how I would feel. I became increasingly anxious over the flight. I felt that I might chicken out, but I knew I had to go because I had put myself through enough pain and regret by missing out on trips in the past. Also, knowing that Paul had paid for the tickets helped my resolve to follow through with the trip. I was not going to leave him hanging, although, knowing Paul, he would have gone anyway and had a great time! He doesn't let anything stop him or get in his way, and he loves to fly. I have learned a lot from him about not living my life in fear.

The day of the flight finally came, and I was ready. Nervous, but ready. I kept wondering whether I would bail at the last minute. The good news is that I boarded that plane despite my fears.

The first flight was about an hour, and it was smooth. The second flight was fine until we began to descend. We started to experience some turbulence while flying through the clouds, so I closed my eyes and rested my head on the tray in front of me. I started humming to distract myself although inside I felt like screaming, *Oh no! Not now!* I turned to Paul who simply looked at me and very nonchalantly said, "It always gets bumpy when you fly through clouds." While I wanted to scream, he was so calm and collected! Then the weirdest thing happened. We landed safely on the runway. *Oh Maritza, another successful landing. You big baby.*

Unfortunately, my first thought after landing wasn't what it should have been, one of pride and happiness for overcoming my fears. Instead, I began to worry about the return flight, whether we would encounter the same dreaded turbulence, and how I might handle that again.

Of course, the trip to Kansas City was absolutely wonderful. Paul and I had a great time walking through the city and attending my friend's beautiful wedding. It was great to catch up with my friend who got married and another friend from high school. Having Paul there made it easier for me to be my authentic self and free of worry. I was happy that I followed through with the trip.

The return flights were smooth. As we landed at the airport back home, I rejoiced within my spirit because I had not allowed my fear to keep me from a great time with good friends. I was finally proud of myself, and I thanked God for allowing me to have a wonderful time. It's like He was saying, "You see, little one? There was never anything to be afraid of. I am always here."

One of the things that people with anxiety don't do enough of is praise or appreciate themselves after they have conquered their fears, even if they are little ones. I hardly ever did that. Instead of embracing the confidence that should follow a victory, I started thinking about future events and how I would survive the next onslaught of emotions. I was still a work in progress.

Chapter Twenty-Two
Finding Mr. Right

I continued to listen to my CDs in the following months, as well as various positive sermons by Pastor Joel Osteen. In one sermon, he gave advice on tending to a financial burden by securing another job if one was able. I thought about this and how much I wanted to pay off my car note sooner, so I took the advice. I applied to work at a local hardware store as a cashier. I had all my evenings free as well as the weekends. My full-time job ended at three every weekday, and I found myself spending my time after work thinking, worrying. I needed a distraction and figured why not get paid to be distracted?

I got the job at a Home Depot. I thanked God and immediately started thinking of how quickly I would pay off my car loan. To be fully honest, there is another reason I wanted to get the job, particularly at a hardware store. To put it frankly, I wanted a husband. I felt ready and wanted to take action over my life. I couldn't find one at church—they were either too young, married, or ordained, so I figured a hardware store was the next best thing. One thing that I heard many pastors preach about is speaking what you want into existence as long as it aligns with God's will.

The Bible says that Jesus came to give us abundant life and freedom through His grace. I was specific in my prayers to find a husband. I wanted a Christian man who would love and accept me as I am.

Joel Osteen says to keep your vision in front of you. I did this by creating a mantra that I repeated as I worked nights cashiering. I would do this while alone at my register, waiting for customers, so no one would think me mad. I knew what I wanted, finally, and I didn't want anyone inserting their thoughts and judgments to try and sway me. Jesus said if you ask anything in His name and believe that it is yours, then it is.

My mantra began: "I'm going to marry a Christian husband who is good and be a singing volcanologist." That last part I know I haven't touched on, but my degree in Geology was always a steppingstone to where I really wanted to go as far as science was concerned which is volcanology or the study of volcanoes. Geology is my second love, but my first, right under Jesus, is singing. I tried to pack all that in a single sentence and said it repeatedly. It may sound crazy but soon enough Prince Charming showed up at my cash register.

One night while working the register in the lumber department, I noticed this handsome, nice-smelling man in the store.

"Hey, how are you? I'm Lawrence and I work here at the Pro Desk." He seemed very friendly and genuine. And, like I said, he smelled good!

"Hi, I'm Maritza, I'm doing well, thanks."

"Have you worked here long?" he asked. "I've never seen you here before."

"Only a few months. I only work nights because I have another job during the day."

"Ah, that's why I've never seen you. Well, it's nice meeting you. Hope we can catch up again soon." And with that he left. Simple, right? Nothing particularly special about our first meeting. I didn't think much of it.

Many weeks passed before I ran into Lawrence again. I had been invited to go to a birthday party one night with some co-workers. We went to a local restaurant where others from the store were waiting. I saw that he was there, but I didn't think much of him other than an acquaintance. We all had a great time, and three weeks later I was invited to another birthday where Lawrence would be.

My coworker and I met Lawrence and his roommate at his place before heading out. We followed behind him since he knew where we were going. After parking our vehicles, we walked into the club and headed for the lounge. As my coworker and his roommate discussed a favorite drink, Lawrence and I walked over toward the music. We were standing up on the mezzanine watching the lights and dancing below.

Leaning on the railing, he confidently asked, "Would you like to go to a movie sometime?"

At that moment, I wasn't sure I was 'feeling' him. I could sense that he liked me. But my friend Tanya was also trying to hook me up with a fellow from her work. We had already exchanged numbers and even though it was very early, I felt that I should concentrate on one guy.

"Thank you but now is not a good time for me," I replied.

"Okay, that's fine," he said. He didn't seem fazed by my answer and was respectful and understanding. We enjoyed the rest of the night dancing and getting to know each other. Then we all went our separate ways home and I didn't hear anything from him until a few weeks later when I got his text.

"Hey, would you like to join me for a movie?" he asked again.

I could sense his friendly smile on the other end of that text. I thought about it and responded, "yes, but as friends?" He agreed. The guy Tanya had introduced me to was too busy to continue to chat with me and I wasn't going to chase any man down, so I let that go and thought to myself, I'm going to give Lawrence a chance. He's been so nice and easygoing with me. Why not?

The following Saturday night we met at the local Regal Cinemas and watched a horrible movie about kids being kidnapped! But we both loved the starring actor. I thought, what kind of a first date movie this is? Throughout the evening I could see Lawrence smiling at me, and he appeared interested.

"Are you having a good time? You look very nice! Thanks for coming out, I love movies and it's nice to meet someone else who does too."

This guy is really into me. Look at the way he is so attentive and always smiling at me. He's so easygoing. He's such a cutie, why didn't I see this before? After the movie, he walked me to my car. He was laughing at what a horrible movie we just saw on a first date. He seemed so happy and was always smiling. I too couldn't stop smiling every time I looked at him. I thought to myself, I must see where this goes.

Soon, we were texting all the time, and he would say the most beautiful things to me. While working at the store the next Saturday, I asked him if he wanted to meet me on my lunch break. He did and brought me chocolates. That next Tuesday, he invited me over to his house and we watched another movie together. He talked throughout the whole movie! I thought, is he ever going to shut up? I knew that I liked him more and was thinking about kissing him to shut him up, but I was nervous. Then, I just went for it! Our first kiss was very nice, and it worked to stop his chatter.

Afterward he put his hand on my knee and the thought came to my mind that he was staking his claim. As I was leaving to go home, he asked me if I wanted to make it official.

"How do you feel about us being official? If you're not ready to call me your boyfriend that's okay. We can take it slow, no problem. I am fine with your decision." He was so easygoing. I smiled at him and said "Yes!" Happy, we kissed again. I got into my car and immediately called Mami.

"Hello?"

"Ma! Guess what? I've got a boyfriend!"

"Ay mija, ya era tiempo! Girl, it's about time!" she replied happily.

We spoke on speaker all the way home. That was of course before it was against the law to be on the phone while driving! I told her all about Lawrence and she listened intently. I felt that this time it was going to be different for me.

Lawrence made me happy. He is loving, kind, compassionate, easygoing and has such a big heart for God. Prior to meeting him, I made a list of the qualities I wanted in my future husband. I put it on the fridge to "keep my vision in front of me," as Joel Osteen recommended. After many weeks of dating, I took down my list of qualities from the refrigerator and marked off all the qualities Lawrence had. I realized God had answered my prayers because all those boxes were checked! He had brought Lawrence into my life, creating him with every quality on my list. I knew the day I wrote that list, God had one just like it in heaven.

I'd finally found someone to love and felt joyful and content! God had finally brought a good man into my life, and I was ever grateful—however, soon I realized I would need Lawrence's strength to lean on during what lay ahead. Again, God knew what

I needed, and He provided. That next fall would test my mental, emotional, and physical health more than ever before.

Chapter Twenty-Three
Death and Destruction

In the late fall of 2014, our relationship was beginning to struggle. Like all courtships, after the novelty phase, the real work sets in. Lawrence and I were increasingly arguing over things I felt were petty yet really frustrated him. He would pick at me for little things, such as using the right knife to cut a certain vegetable. I told him he was being too sensitive. A knife is a knife and if it cuts, use it. But the more he fussed at me the more I wanted to be alone, until one day I realized he wasn't angry with me, he was concerned about his parents as they were experiencing health problems.

Still, he would get easily agitated with me and I was growing increasingly tired of it. I had stress in my life as well. I was still trying to take better care of myself, learning how to see the light at the end of the tunnel and avoiding the dark cloud of depression. I knew I would get there, even if it meant spending a few days away from Lawrence. We were spending most of our time together, and even though I loved and adored him, I needed some space to let my anger out, without it affecting him. I knew we would become stronger as a couple, and that whether he realized it or not, he needed time for himself as well. We had been dating for over a year and I believed we would one day marry, but first, we had to deal with our own issues.

I refused to take old habits into a marriage. After living through all the fighting between my parents, I knew I desired something different, something better. Also, I respected and loved us both too much to let that happen. After all, marriage would introduce its own issues into our lives. We didn't need to add to them.

Then a fifteen-year-old girl that was part of my church community was brutally murdered in her home while trying to protect her family from an assailant who may have been mentally disturbed. I didn't know the details. My church performed the memorial service, and I sang with the choir. I did not know her, but I felt her loss just the same. The service was heartbreaking of course, especially when her twin sister stood at the podium and thanked everyone for coming. She seemed to struggle as she walked, but I wasn't sure if it was from grief or from the attack on her family. All of this was terribly sad, and I could hardly bear it.

Throughout the service, the choir sang songs of God's love and peace. As we sang, I looked to the young girl's mother, who was holding up an oxygen mask to her face. I couldn't even imagine what she was feeling—she seemed overwhelmed too. The music we sang didn't help me cope with the sadness I was feeling, and I immediately regretted telling Lawrence not to come. His presence would have helped me breathe. After the service, I drove to his place, and I told him so. I know I had told him before he didn't have to come but I was wrong. I needed him. He held me for a while as I quietly sobbed into his shirt.

Just before the news of the young girl's death, I was browsing social media and saw a post from the mother of one of my friends that seemed desperate. She was reaching out to her daughter's friends in hope that one of them might have heard from her since she was unsuccessful at reaching her. My friend, Isla, also suffers from depression. I had reached out to her in the past for support and encouragement because our struggles were very similar and we could relate to one another. When I saw her mother's plea on social media for any information about her daughter, I grew fearful of the possibilities and tried to reach out to her by phone.

When she didn't respond, I left a message. I followed through with texts and a personal message on social media. I told her how much she meant to me. I finally reached out to her husband and then received a response saying she was okay. I was glad to hear that but still felt a growing concern for her. I asked how he and the kids were doing, and he said they were all fine, but his short answer had me feeling maybe I needed to give them space, so I apologized. I understood they were going through something personal, and I wanted to tread lightly.

I respected the fact that whatever it was, it was a family issue. I just wanted Isla to tell me that she was okay. I reached out to a mutual friend of ours and she also assured me that Isla was fine. But this wasn't enough for me. I knew what depression was and Isla wasn't talking to me. I gave it time. For a while we lost connection, and I missed her.

Many months later, I deactivated my social media account, but I would still check for news on Isla through Mami's account. I wanted to see if she was doing better and how her life was. I couldn't call because for some reason, I no longer had her number. I remembered when I was going through my darkest days, I didn't want anyone to know about it. My depression, in the past, made me feel like I was a burden, so I didn't reach out to my friends. I could only imagine what Isla thought or what she was going through. Not being in contact with her hurt, but that was not her fault. I began to think I would never hear from her again, and this left me with great sorrow. *Did I do something wrong? No. Think! You know what it's like to go through this. You wanted your space. Give her the same.* I felt that maybe I had done something wrong in our friendship and, unnecessarily, I took that sorrow into my heart.

Thankfully, as time went by, we did reconnect. I told her I was praying for her all that time while we were disconnected and that I missed her. She told me that she had met someone during that hard time that reminded her of me. This new friend brought her some comfort and maybe that was how my prayers were answered. I thought how beautiful are the ways of God that He would connect us in such a way, that my silent prayers would cross great distances and bring her comfort through a total stranger. I am learning more and more to trust the people I love to God. He always knows what He is doing. He restored us to each other after a time and I give Him all the Glory.

It was almost the Thanksgiving holiday and we decided to spend it with Mami and Ariana in Virginia that year. But just before we left for Mami's house, we met up with another good friend of mine, Isabelle, for her birthday dinner at P.F. Chang's in Baltimore. We went with a group of her friends, and we all sat together at a long table chatting while we waited for our mutual friend Kelly and her husband to arrive.

"Happy birthday, girlie!" I said happily.

"Thanks!" Isabelle responded, smiling.

We had met years ago working for the same geotechnical company along with Tanya and we all instantly hit it off. Isabelle's birthday is right before Thanksgiving, and we celebrated together that year. It was like having two feasts! Kelly and her husband finally arrived a few minutes before we ordered. She was almost nine months pregnant, and concern filled her face.

"Sorry, we're late guys. My family has been trying to find my sister. She's been missing and we're not sure where she is." She said wearily. She appeared worried and exhausted. "That's why we ran late coming here."

We were all shocked to hear the news and I immediately wanted to connect with her in some way, so I silently prayed for her sister's safe return. After dinner, on the way home, I thought about Kelly's sister. *What if Mary or Ariana went missing? I'd be pulling my hair out!* I cannot remember if it was days or weeks later when the news came about Kelly's sister. Her life was taken from her and the family was shocked and in deep mourning. And again, I took it all in, into the very core of my heart.

The authorities were involved and there was an investigation into the death of Kelly's sister. How did anybody get through something like that? I never told Kelly how I felt about the passing of her sister until years later over a phone call. We shed tears together and I was so sorry I didn't tell her sooner that my heart broke for her. What do you tell someone going through that? During that horrible time, I wondered if my prayers were enough for her. I kept thinking, what if I'd lost one of my sisters that way? I couldn't bear it! At the time, I only desired to comfort her in some way, but not knowing how left me feeling like an inadequate friend.

Stress can wreak havoc on your body, regardless of how much you try to avoid it. Sometime after the deaths of the young girl at my church and of Kelly's sister, I woke up one morning with a red bump under my left eyebrow. A few days later, I felt my lymph nodes swell up by my ear and on my neck. I went to the doctor to find out that I had developed Shingles. He prescribed Amoxicillin for me, which ended up giving me another infection, for which the doctor prescribed another medication. The Shingles caused migraines and a horrible, itchy rash on the left side of my head. Geez! What else could go wrong? I wondered.

Lawrence and I drove to Mami's to spend Thanksgiving with her and Ariana. After eating a delicious turkey and all the trimmings, I went to lie down because I had developed another splitting headache.

"Maritza? How are you feeling?" Mami asked.

I lay in Abuelita's old bed in complete darkness, facing the wall. The pain was piercing my brain.

"Do you want to go to the hospital?" she asked.

"Yeah, I think I should." Then I started to grow fearful that the pain could mean something else. I ended up in the emergency room that evening. *What if this pain is cancer or something? Oh God, please take it away.*

The doctor confirmed that it was still the Shingles virus and not some other terrible thing for which I was thankful. I was prescribed more meds and afterward, Mami drove us back to her house.

The next day I told Lawrence we needed to get out, so that evening we went to see a movie. It was one of the spin-offs of the DreamWorks movie, Madagascar. This one was about the penguins. We laughed so much that I felt my spirits rise again. After the movie we decided to go to a local grocery store to pick up some things we needed.

As we were finishing up in the grocery line, I got a call from my brother Joshua, asking me if I heard the news.

"Hey, where are you guys?" he asked.

"We are just leaving Kroger's. We saw a movie and are headed home. Why what's up?"

"Uncle Joseph died."

I was silent for a second as the news sunk in. Uncle Joseph was sick with the flu and Mami had called him to check in on him a few days before Thanksgiving.

"What? Ok, we're headed back now!"

I grabbed our bags off the checkout line belt and told Lawrence that we needed to rush back.

"What's wrong, love?"

"My uncle just died," I replied, my thoughts racing. We hurried to the car and took off for Mami's house.

When we got back, Mami was already making calls to the family. I didn't get a chance to tell her I was sorry. She was already in "take-care-of-everything" mode. Watching her be so "on it" and not cry broke something inside me.

Mami later told me she knew something was wrong when she couldn't reach her brother again after the last time they spoke. She had contacted the police in New York, the closest precinct to his apartment, and asked if they could do a wellness check on him.

"That last conversation, he was so sick, I heard death in his voice," she said as she stared off into space. He had told her that he was waiting for his ex's family to take the kids for the holiday, and then he would go to the doctor.

The NYPD did find him. In his chair, deceased. Mami told me that Uncle Joseph had not gotten the flu shot that year as he always did, and ended up dying from its complications.

"I think he held on until the family came to pick up the kids. Then I think he let go," Mami said.

My uncle had two small children who were going to spend the holiday with their mother's family—they would never see their dad again.

"He knew he was dying." All I could do was look at her, helplessly. Poor Mami. It was just too much for me to bear.

With all of this going on, the deaths of the young girl at church, Kelly's sister, my beloved uncle, and the loss of communication with Isla at the time, I was on an emotional overload. My entire life I have always empathized with what others were going through. I wanted them to know I was always there for them, and I felt their pain as well. I wanted to please them, but also, I just naturally cared a lot about people and their struggles. I tended to wear my heart on my sleeve, and although I had lived through some hard times, I continued to care for others even more. I'm glad my heart had not been hardened by the tough times. Still, I felt my anxiety and depression ramping up with all of this.

When Uncle Joseph died, Mami went into her "I-got-this, I'm-taking-care-of-everything" mode, per usual. She went to New York and met up with her other brother, Uncle James, for a week and they began to sort out Uncle Joseph's insurance and pension paperwork, only to find out neither existed. Both were saddened and extremely frustrated. She later went to his apartment and found his wallet and its contents thrown all over the floor as if someone had gone through it looking for something. In his wallet was a picture of me. I couldn't recall the last time I'd seen him. Now, Mami hadn't even the time herself to grieve because she immediately started taking care of his affairs and planning to lay him to rest.

Uncle Joseph's service was held at the same funeral home in the Bronx where Uncle Angel's and my grandparents' services were held years earlier. Out of five, now only three were left from Abuelita's and Papi Chi's children: Mami, Uncle James, and Uncle Tony. Uncle Tony lived out on the west coast with his family. No matter the distance, the siblings greatly felt the loss of their older brother. I walked into the familiar place of the funeral parlor and memories flooded back of when we laid to rest my other family members. Uncle James met me in the parlor.

"How ya doing, kid?" he asked as he kissed my cheek in greeting.

"I'm okay," I said sadly as I let my head rest on his shoulder.

"It's gonna be okay." He reassured me, tightening his hug.

There was no money and no will, so Uncle Joseph's closest friend, Roger, paid for everything. Mami felt obligated to pay him back but didn't have any money at the time, which stressed her even more. My heart broke for her. She always had to take care of everyone and now she felt obligated to repay my uncle's friend when she had other things that needed financial attention in her life. I don't even know if Mami ever got the chance to mourn her older brother's passing.

So of course, I took it all in, her selfless acts while she ignored her heart, her sadness, and frustration. I took it all into my heart. It's okay, Mami. It's all over. You can cry now.

Chapter Twenty-Four
Down, but Not Out

November 30, 2015, I was looking on a travel website for tickets to Europe. Both Joshua and Ezra were stationed in Europe, and we wanted to go visit them. However, travel was still an issue for me. Even though I struggled to fly, I still liked to look online for tickets. Mami and I were on the phone, and she was doing the same. She had already purchased hers and Ariana's tickets. We had talked about visiting my brothers for some time. While talking, she found a good deal for a non-stop ticket from Philly to London for under nine hundred dollars She told me to go to the website that she was looking at, but my computer kept freezing.

"I'll get it for you if you can't," she offered.

I was wary, fidgety, and anxious.

"No, it's okay, mom. I want Lawrence to go too, but we don't have enough money to go."

"If you let this go, the price will go up. This is a good deal."

"I know," I said wearily, anxiety and sadness swelling.

So, while immobilized by technical difficulties and fear, Mami went ahead and bought them and told me after the fact. I was going on this trip and there was no backing out like I had done in the past.

From that moment until the trip, my anxiety was off the Richter scale. There were many days I was close to having a panic attack, which I hadn't had for a few years. But despite my progress in keeping the attacks at bay, I remembered how intense the feelings could get, and to my surprise, I still harbored a great amount of fear towards them. I discovered I still did not trust myself as much as I thought I did. When the scary thoughts came, I became increasingly nervous, due to the overwhelming power they had over me.

I began seeing my therapist again and he told me to start "looking at" or observing my thoughts and learn to be patient again.

I felt like a liar that I was again swimming in my anxiety. It began to depress me—I thought I had been further along in my progress. So, I figured, one more time, let's do this all the way holding nothing back, following all the rules while being true to myself. The first thing I had to do was remember to trust God. Then, observe and keep my judgmental comments about what I saw in my mind to myself. The reel played something like this:

Okay, okay, let's start at the beginning. What do you feel?

Scared.

Why?

What if I have a panic attack on the plane and go crazy? What if I can't get out?

I don't think you'd want to get out of a plane that is in motion. It's the safest place to be when traveling. It's safer than driving. People fly every day. You can do this. Keep telling yourself this.

I hated that I still feared the symptoms of the nervousness and anxiety, and that my real fear was total loss of bodily and mental functions. I feared that this would happen, and I would not be able to bring myself back to reality, and I'd become stuck. I still had an issue with remaining in my comfort zone. I knew I needed to come to a place where I believed I was my own safe place, but I was not quite there. Anger filled me realizing this was still going on, and I put pressure on myself like I had done in the past, to "get well" faster.

Apparently, my tires were still spinning at the bottom of that icy hill. I was angry because this journey had been long enough, and it should be over by now. I felt defeated. Believe me, life was better at this moment than it had been years prior, but there was still quite an amount of fear left and it was holding onto me. People say that anxiety and depression are a part of life, but that makes their effects sound so trivial.

In the months leading up to the trip, I began waking up with the familiar nervous feeling. But I remembered what Dr. Claire Weekes said in her book, Hope and Healing for Your Nerves—that just because you have a bad morning doesn't mean you will have a bad day. That is very true because no matter how nervous I was in the morning, my day always ended up getting better. She also said in her book that when you wake with the nervous feeling, get out of bed! Don't stay there and stew in your discomfort. Get up, get dressed, and get the day started. As a bed-loving, sleeping-in person, I struggled with this, but once I decided to do it, getting out of bed really helped. On my bad days I'd say, Maritza, I know you have anxiety but sometimes you just have to get your butt out there! I'd smile afterward, and I would feel better.

Sometimes, you have to make fun of yourself, loosen up. *Oh my gosh, Maritza! Why all the dramatics? It's just a trip. You act as if you were traveling to the moon!*

I learned to look at my accomplishments during my dark times and say, *Go 'head, girl! You know you got this! You're still here! It hasn't gotten the best of you yet!* And then I smile again.

In my determination to squash my anxious feelings, I'd grab whatever resource I could to assist me, as if I was hurriedly taking ingredients from a grocery shelf to make a last-minute dinner for an unexpected guest. One of my resources was my local radio station, Shine 95.1 FM. I'd listen to it a lot, and it seemed like every other song relayed exactly what I was feeling. This reminded me God had not forgotten me, and this comforted me. I reminded myself every day was another opportunity to trust God more, to be encouraged in my discouragement, to really depend on Him for everything. I think this is what He has been telling me all that time. To give it all to Him.

On Easter in 2016, I'd gotten sick with a cold. It was so bad that I had to miss an entire week of work. The regular cold symptoms began—dizziness, congestion, and body aches. I saw the doctor on Easter Sunday, and he gave me some cough medicine and a note to stay home from work the next day. I had no idea it would get worse.

That evening after seeing the doctor, my temperature rose to 103 degrees, and I began worrying about it getting higher. I had no energy to go back to the doctor at that point. Then, as if on schedule, my anxiety kicked in. Fear washed over me, and I began sobbing like a child. Between my anxiety increasing, the uncontrollable crying, and being so sick, I finally had to admit it—depression had arrived yet again. With no strength left and my defenses down, I was totally left open to negative thoughts. Exposed and vulnerable, I could not combat them.

I had thoughts of breaking up with Lawrence because I didn't want to burden him. That's what depression does. It subtracts good things from life while the anxiety adds limitations.

Look at you! Here again. Pitiful. You never learn. Lawrence doesn't deserve this. Let him go.

I was to the point where I began losing my faith. I felt I didn't have anything left to hold on to. I thought, why would God let this happen to me, again? Maybe He did exist, but maybe He didn't truly care about me after all. He's too busy with other things. He's helped you long enough and you didn't learn anything. Maybe He doesn't even see you.

Suddenly, a vision of me being suspended in midair came to me. I was in an unknown city, floating in the air between the skyscrapers. The day was sunny, with no clouds in the sky. A beautiful spring day was taking place beneath me as I floated high up without a care about what was going on. Despite there being multiple buildings to grab onto, they were too far for me to reach. I was too tired to reach out, to grab hold of anything, so I just hovered in the air parallel to the earth beneath me, as if I were lying on a bed, ready to fall. But I didn't fall, instead, there was a great large hand holding me. My arms flung open wide and hung over each side of the hand. My head almost drooped over the middle finger. My body perfectly fit into the center of the palm. My face, masked in complete exhaustion, my eyes too tired to blink. I couldn't hold on, but Someone was holding on to me.

Some months earlier at church, I had come to the altar after Mass. With tears forming in my eyes, I'd asked God not to let me go no matter what happened, even if I let go. I never imagined that months later, I would be at the point of losing my faith in God. How could I know I would again be in a dark place and not have the energy to cry out to Him? Nevertheless, He heard my prayer, and His hand held me so that I would not fall. He told me that it was okay that I let go, He was always holding onto me.

I think sometimes He has to get us there for us to learn that He has total control, and we can always trust Him with anything.

I learned what it meant to really depend on Him, completely and totally, like a small child depends on his parents. When I could not hold on, He held onto me and only He had enough strength and faith for both of us.

I told Lawrence everything I was feeling and that I had thoughts of breaking up with him. He gently reminded me I was not alone in this and that he would stand by me. He told me we would get through it together, and we did.

I went back to listening to my CDs again and realized that anxiety can cause extremely unpleasant feelings like dissociation and fainting. Even though I knew this happened to me in the past, I felt like I was experiencing it all for the first time. It was particularly hard for me to go to work feeling that way. In the past, I would miss days of work but I told myself this time had to be different.

Okay, what are you thinking?

What if I faint today at work? I'm by myself in the office. Who would know?

You are not going to faint. It's going to be okay.

I feel bad.

Of course, you do, you've been sick.

I'm going to be like this all week!

No, you are not. You will get through this. You are stronger than you know. You've gotten through it before, and you'll get through it again.

Chapter Twenty-Five
Happy Horizon

Finally, the day of the trip to Europe arrived. Lawrence and Mary and I were scheduled to fly out of Philadelphia together and had an hour-and-a-half drive ahead of us. The flight was scheduled to leave in the evening, so I had time to run some errands.

Mami and Ariana were already with Ezra in England, waiting for us. As I drove with Mary, who was helping me with my errands, the thought of the approaching airplane ride floated in the back of my mind. I was able to keep the nervousness away by staying busy, but the anticipation of it was still there. Around noon, Mary and I stopped at a Chick-Fil-A for lunch.

I can't believe I have an appetite and I'm not yet nervous! We leave tonight! I'm so glad I won't be traveling alone. I wish we were there already!

Soon, it was time to load up and head north. I drove because I felt better when I was in control of something. After we parked and unloaded the car, we waited for the bus to take us to the terminal. *Okay, so far so good! I think I'm getting excited! Oh boy, here comes the bus!*

We soon arrived at the ticket counter, and everything seemed to be going smoothly. I had finally begun to feel the excitement that had eluded me all year. In the beginning, I was so scared but now all I could think about was being in Europe with my family and Lawrence. My excitement began to grow, and I was even looking forward to getting on the plane! I had England in my sights and with each step I took, I felt closer than before. Remember, one foot in front of the other.

The text messages from Mami and Ariana enjoying themselves with Ezra increased my yearning to go more than ever. Later, Mary described my excitement as leading the army because I was in front of her and Lawrence telling them, "Come on! Let's go!" I could barely contain myself! I half-ran, half-skipped to the gate, excited like a giddy child.

Finally, we handed over our tickets to be scanned and I walked down the bridge to the plane. *Alright Maritza, you're almost there. You're doing good.* Before stepping over the threshold onto the plane, I did something then that I still do today. I took my finger and made the sign of the cross on the outside of the plane. I then stepped into the plane, turned, and looked down the long aisle. *It's go time now, girl.*

Once we found our seats my boldness continued to surprise me as I sat by the window. I normally chose the aisle seat in case my nerves make me need to use the bathroom. Again, a little semblance of control is everything to us anxious travelers! But once the door was shut and the plane started to move, I began to feel that I might bolt up in a frenzied panic and scream to let me out. That white-hot adrenaline began to course through my veins. *This is the test, hon.*

I felt the panic mounting. I heard myself scream inside so I decided to take a Xanax. I only usually took those when I was on a plane to help calm me down. Initially, I wanted to take half of one but when I bit down to halve it, it came apart in my mouth, so I decided to just take the entire thing. I don't know if that was smart, taking it in pieces. But let me tell you what those little pieces did—they gave me an instant reaction. I was calmed down to the point of falling asleep. As the wheels of the plane jerked us forward, I closed my eyes and let myself go. Then it came, the moment of takeoff, and there was no turning back.

The wheels began to race forward and suddenly I became brave. In spite of myself, I recited quietly, "Faster! Do it faster!" Soon I felt that familiar feeling of the wheels lifting off the ground and we were in the air. It was over. I had done it, the hard part anyway. I was in the air, between heaven and earth. I let myself feel what I was feeling, even when the light turbulence occurred. I just sat there, breathing, and looking at the monitor in front of me. The monitor depicted where we were on a map, our speed, and the countdown of the time until landing in London. Watching the hours countdown to landing gave me a feeling of control, however minute but it was enough for me. But as calm as I felt, I still could not sleep, no matter how tired the pill made me. When I did try to sleep, I was stirred awake by the turbulence. It was like the plane was fooling around with me. Wake up, girlie! Look outside!

I opened the window shade and stared into the distance, captivated by the blue-black sky and a blanket of soft white clouds beneath us. The moon was full and in my direct line of vision. It looked so beautiful. Lawrence and Mary were asleep along with the other passengers. I sat in the stillness of the night and realized how truly blessed I was. *Not even the birds get to enjoy this view. Not so bad huh, Maritza? What were you so afraid of? Silly girl.*

The rest of the flight was peaceful. I kept looking out the window, but whenever there was a little shake of the plane, I'd slam down the window shade as if to say, okay there's enough of that! Only so much bravery for one night!

As we entered UK airspace, my excitement returned to me. I pulled up the window shade again and peered down below to Europe greeting us. As we began our descent, my eyes were glued to the ground that was slowly coming toward us. I knew that in mere minutes it would be all over and I would have lived through another flight. I was very excited for the wheels to touch down and when they did, I exclaimed in a whisper, "Yes!" and made a fist and punched the air—I'd done it! I was back on the ground, this time in England. Another one bites the dust!

We went through customs and the gentleman working there was very friendly which further put me at ease. As we left customs and came through some doors, Mami and Ezra were standing there smiling, waiting for us. Mami took pictures of us with her phone and posted on social media, "My girls arriving in London!"

Lawrence was so excited to be in Europe! He had not traveled much outside of the United States so there were a lot of firsts for him to experience. We loaded our luggage in the rented van and as Ezra drove us to his house, I gazed out of the window at the quaint British homes and roads. We were not in London proper, but that didn't matter to me because what made those things special was that they were in England, and finally, so were we. We arrived at his house to see Ariana waiting for us and we had a nice dinner and relaxed, taking photos of all of us together.

The next day we took a trip to Stonehenge and then to Bath. At Stonehenge, I was starting to feel a little weak from some anxiety, so I bought some soup and a sandwich. There was a bus that took visitors to the site from the visitor's center, but people also had the option to walk and that is what Lawrence and I did with Ezra and Mary. Mami and Ariana took the bus. During the walk, I ate my food at leisure and reminded myself all was well. *It's okay, you're just feeling traveling anxieties. Remember, anxiety poses as excitement, too, so think of it that way instead. You're with your family and you're going to be okay.*

I breathed, letting those positive thoughts sink in, and began to relax as we walked. Soon, the relaxation was replaced with heavy breathing and blood rushing. Not because the anxiety got worse, but because the walk turned into a marathon! I had no idea the walk would be so long. When we finally arrived at the site, breathing heavily after the half-hour hike, Mami and Ariana were sitting down and ready to head back.

"Oh my gosh, what took you so long? I'm glad we didn't walk! We already saw everything and are ready to go back." Mami joked.

Ugh. I'm taking the bus back. But after all that walking, I'm going to take my time here.

I couldn't believe that I was at Stonehenge. I had seen documentaries on it and photos never imagining in my wildest dreams I would one day be here. I stood in awe, observing the large, timeless stones. All around me were smooth green, silky hills, and not a quarry in site. As I think of it now, it was almost like being at a crossroads where I was transitioning from my anxious past to my peaceful present.

In Genesis 28:10-22, Jacob sets up a pillar in Bethel to commemorate a powerful vision of God and not to forget what God had given him. In Joshua 4:1-8 God commanded the Israelites to cross the River Jordan which He miraculously stopped so that they could. They then erected stones in the Promised Land in a place called Gilgal as a memorial to God's love and miraculous help. In 1 Samuel 7:7-12, after God led the Israelites into victory from the Philistines, Samuel erects a large stone and named it "Ebenezer," meaning "the stone of help." Samuel wanted to publicly declare in a permanent way what God had done for them.

As we walked around the circle of stones, I took in every detail. From the blue-gray stone pillars to the contrast of the emerald, green grass and the lighter gray overcast clouds above, there was no question about the history of this place—and I was beginning to walk out of the history of my struggle with anxiety. Each pillar or stone has a story, but for me, each represented a milestone in my life with anxiety.

The first was realizing I needed help and the second was getting that help. The third was opening up and learning not to feel ashamed, the fourth was learning to be patient with myself. The fifth and sixth were about coming to love myself closer to the way God does. The seventh and eighth, the breaking of strongholds in my life such as fear and guilt—learning to see them for what they truly are—lies. The ninth, appreciation of my triumphs and a growing peace within my heart. The tenth stone was fallen over and this one was the most significant. It was the end of all the struggles and where the top of the head of the pillar pointed was my new path to freedom. The rest of them I took as milestones to take place in my future such as marriage, children, becoming debt free, and many more adventures ahead of me. I believe these are the things God has for me because I have asked them of Him. I imagine many visitors come away from Stonehenge feeling differently. I know that I did.

Next stop: Paris. We took the Eurostar from London into Paris where we were set to meet up with Joshua. Once we cleared the tunnel, the fields of France surrounded us. The love and awe I felt continued to grow. Looking around to see Ezra and Mami, Lawrence and Ariana seated behind me and Mary, I thought about how blessed we all were.

Soon the train came to a gradual halt at the station, Gare de l'Est, or East Gate. We met up with Joshua at the station who traveled from Germany to meet us. He walked up casually with a big smile wearing his newsboy cap.

"Sup guys?" he said with a welcoming grin.

We all hugged each other, smiles around for miles!

It was so good to be together again. After checking into our hotel, we decided to book a bus tour. One of our stops was the famous cathedral, Notre Dame. Lawrence was so taken with it he claimed it as his church.

"Now this is MY church! It's so awesome!" he exclaimed. I just laughed at his childlike giddiness.

We hopped on the bus again and stopped at the next place everyone goes to see in France—Le Tour Eiffel! The large brown, towering structure reaches almost to Heaven—the icon of Paris. The seven of us gathered right beneath it and took a selfie with the camera pointed up into the interior of the tower. It's one of our most memorable family photos! We spent two glorious days in Paris, and I didn't realize how many darn Eiffel Towers we bought until we got home!

The next destination on our family trip was Germany, to visit Joshua's home. Ezra and Joshua, both living in Europe, had international driver's licenses, so each drove a car and we split up between the two. We planned a trip to our old childhood home in Veitshochhiem and then drove off to Luxembourg.

Lawrence got to experience life on the autobahn for the first time and loved it. Once we saw the white road sign with the three black lines that indicated no speed limit, Joshua took off! We got up to 160.9km/hr or a hundred miles per hour. At this point now, I had become very comfortable and wasn't bothered by any nervousness. I enjoyed seeing places for the first time with Lawrence to whom Europe was completely new.

Next was a drive into Switzerland, where we crashed a street party in Zurich! The city was just as amazing as Paris, with its blue-green river, stone homes with multi-colored flower baskets adorning the windows, water fountains where people could fill up their water bottles, and countless quaint shops that lined the cobblestone streets. People flooded the streets as they walked over toward the water where a concert was taking place. Families, couples, and single people with backpacks on from every part of the area enjoyed life together as the music played. We walked and walked, snapping more pictures, and buying even more souvenirs.

After a few hours, we were back in the cars and headed to our hotel in the small yet stunning country of Liechtenstein. We headed south seeing more of Switzerland. The countryside was incredible. Houses and sheep dotted the green hills almost all the way up into the base of the rocky range that is the Swiss Alps.

After our road trip, we checked into our hotel and went up to our rooms. Each room had a balcony and a stunning view of the country. The mountain range cradled a small green valley below where many homes dotted the flat earth, and the river curved and zigzagged through the rest of the small country. From our elevation, I felt as if I could reach out and touch a cloud.

That evening we dined like royalty! Mami treated us to a fare of steak and potatoes and greens at a local restaurant. Everyone but me and Mami sampled the local beer and relaxed after our long trip. The restaurant had the same amazing view as the hotel. The side of the restaurant where we were seated overhung the mountain and added an extra "awe" effect to the scenery. I thought to myself, how could I ever doubt that God loved me? Look at where He has brought me. I couldn't believe I was so scared to get on that plane, but I am so grateful that I did!

That evening, on the balcony after dinner, surrounded by the Alps and the glittering lights of the homes below us, stars above,

Lawrence asked for my hand in marriage. I said yes and the rest, they say, is history!

It's amazing how stepping into faith even when you are in fear, great things can happen. To be surrounded by family in some of the most beautiful places on Earth with the man I love was incredible. It was my miracle. I finally found my freedom.

Soon it was time to get back on the plane and go home, and while I had some general nervousness about the return trip, it turned out to be not too bad at all. The flight was good, but an hour before we landed the captain came over the speaker:

"Folks, we've been informed from flights ahead of us to expect some turbulence so please return to your seats and fasten your seatbelts." *Really? We were doing so well!* I kept my Bible with me, reading scripture verses that spoke about not being afraid, as I usually do when I travel. Then I put it down in my bag and just breathed. Soon the plane began to shake, and I held onto the armrests. Lawrence took my hand and Mary, who was seated behind us, reached over, and patted my shoulder for added reassurance. During the turbulence, I remembered a saying in a particular sermon that all I have to do is say, "Jesus," and He is instantly with me. In my fear, I half-whispered, half-cried out, "Jesus!" When it was over, I realized if I could get through this, I could get on a plane again. And I knew Lawrence and I were headed home to start our lives together.

Epilogue

It's amazing to me to finally be here, looking out from the dark tunnel of anxiety and depression to the light of peace and complete joy. I decided to end my story the same way it began—with comparison.

Comparison has stolen my joy since I was five. After many years, I finally decided to dedicate time to break this bad habit. In the summer of 2017, just before Lawrence and I were about to be married in October, I made a pact with myself to do just that. I began to focus my energy and thoughts on being comparison-free. Of course, it took a few years of strong commitment, but I didn't allow that to deter me. After all, it took many more years to cement this bad habit. I just needed a jackhammer of positive affirming thoughts to break through the thick concrete of negative speech that held the fuel to my constant companions—anxiety and depression.

I believed that deep down, this struggle was going to end with me and not affect the next generation. I got brutally honest with myself one evening—I had to have total acceptance of and thankfulness for my struggle if I was ever going to see the end of it. Once I was able to thank God for the struggle, the chains began to fall off.

I can confidently say that on the morning of July 6, 2021, on my way to work and in mid-prayer, thanking God that I would be released from the grip of comparison, I felt something lift off of my chest. I knew instantly that comparison was now a part of my past and no longer my present—as long as I stayed in His Word.

The Lord, Jesus Christ brings healing every day to those who ask it of Him and believe that He can and will do it. From my experience, it most likely will not happen in your time, when you want it, but it will happen.

Now, when I am around women to whom I used to compare myself, and who, to me, took up every ounce of energy in the room and left me to feel like the smallest crumb, I look at them with love and know there is no comparison, no envy. I know who I am and Whose I am. I am proud of myself and the woman the Lord has grown me to be. And you can be, too.

I now look forward to the future, rather than fear it. I look forward to learning new skills and mastering my job. I look forward to new trips, new people, and my life with Lawrence at my side. When I think about the future, I get excited about all the great things I can experience that make life worth living.

I continue to put into practice everything I have learned throughout my journey and continue to be open to learning more. I know deep down I will always take care of myself, and I trust myself. Life is full of anxieties and sad moments, but also full of exciting and happy ones. It's okay to feel sadness but don't let it hold you back. I like to think of emotions as seasons. For me, sad emotions are like winter and late fall, happy ones like summer and spring. After winter comes spring. That's a comforting thought.

God has done extraordinary things in my life in the face of my anxiety. I was afraid anxiety would keep me from them, but God has shown me this is not the case. In fact, He is using my past experiences with anxiety and depression to improve my life by sharing my story with others. I finally know my purpose and that my life has meaning.

Author's Note

Sometime back in 2015, I decided to write about my life with depression and anxiety. I didn't think anything would come from it—it was just for therapeutic purposes. As I wrote, I was able to see through the thought patterns I had and the behaviors that resulted. In this, I learned more about myself.

For instance, every time there was a big change in my life—starting classes at Towson University, Mami moving away to Richmond, going on the European trip—my anxieties would be triggered by being overwhelmed by the situation. Depression would soon follow as would my lack of confidence that I could deal with it all. Was it because of the trauma I experienced growing up? Did living with the constant fighting and worrying somehow damage my self-confidence? I think that it contributed.

Every big life change and even the times leading up to it made me question whether or not I could handle it, or better yet, live through it. No one can handle it all and that's okay. God had to take me through each trial and season to show me that I could and would make it through. Each depressive and anxious moment did strengthen me and helped me to grow.

The traumatic experiences growing up could have also led to my brain not being able to retain information well, which may be why I struggled so much to focus during college. I learned that between the ages of three and eighteen, a person's brain will develop the personality that he or she will have for the rest of his or her life. If hardships occur during those years, as the brain is developing, those hardships or traumas could affect it. That made sense to me. Because I worried and was in constant "fight or flight mode," it's possible there was little room for anything else, like my studies, to take precedence in my brain. There are great books, such as Body Keeps the Score by Bessel van der Kolk, that scientifically explain what cortisol, the adrenaline-pumping, fight or flight response does to the body over time. In his work, van der Kolk explores the impact of trauma on humans and the relationship between experiencing trauma and suffering from mental health disorders.

Writing this memoir helped me learn either peace or depression awaits on the other side of a panic attack. I choose peace, and I must continue to choose it every day.

Sometimes, I wonder if I had gone on those missed trips out west and to Puerto Rico and Texas, would I have followed a different path? In other words, did my past decisions, often dictated by fear, cause me to miss out on God's original plan for my life? What memories would have been made if I hadn't missed that trip to Puerto Rico during my family reunion? What friends might I have made had I followed through with the university trip? I realize now that this kind of thinking is living in the past, and I refuse to cling to that guilt anymore.

There is this practice of forgiveness and letting go, which I am experimenting with. It allows you to move forward into new, fresh beginnings rather than remain stuck with past hurts and disappointments. Maybe I was supposed to go through all the things that I did because if I didn't, I wouldn't be writing this now. You wouldn't be reading this now. Nothing can hinder God's plan for our lives, not anxiety or depression or anything. His Will is always done. I believe if we stay in the present, we can help avoid and or at least lessen guilt and anxiety. This has always been my goal—even though at times it has seemed so far away.

One thing would bring me back every time—and that was music. I remember the day I came home from school and saw on the news that Selena was shot and killed at a Days Inn in Texas. I didn't get to know much about her before she died but I do remember seeing her on TV. Every night of the week, my family would gather in the den and watch "Dos Mujeres Un Camino" (Two Women, One Way). It was a famous Mexican telenovela back in the mid-nineties. Selena played a cameo in the show as a love interest for one of the male characters who was in a band. All I remember of the scene was that the gentleman was behind Selena's character, and Selena turned around and smiled her famous, red-lipped smile at him. She wore a black cowboy hat and looked glamorous! Fast forward to that day after school, in total disbelief, all I could say was "wow." She was gone.

I bought her English album and loved it right away. As always, I pressed my ear against my radio speaker and closed my eyes, and let the music flow into me. I was taken by her raw talent and style of singing. As long as the music played, I could forget about the fighting in the house. I loved Selena's voice and began mimicking her style. I bought every album of hers I could find at the PX (Military Post Xchange) between living in Maryland in my high school years and when we moved to Washington. Whatever new or old music of Selena's was out, I had to have it.

Soon, I had almost all her music and most of her songs memorized. I wanted to sing again because of Selena. I had sung on my own and for a few people as a young girl and was told by others that I was good. By ninth and tenth grade, all I could think about when I came home from school was turning on my radio and singing with Selena. Music helped me get through the toughest years at home. The more I listened to her, the more I loved her...and mourned her.

One night, I had a dream about her. We were at a burger joint or some fast-food place. She was on the other side of the counter as if she were going to take my order. I began sobbing and she immediately came running toward me. She wore a white top and white jeans. Her raven hair was slicked back in a ponytail, which fell behind her in waves. She had her iconic hoops and red lipstick on. As she came towards me, jumping over the counter, hands on one side as she swung her legs over to greet me, she landed in front of me. She brought her face in line with mine and pinched my cheeks the way an aunt would pinch the cheeks of her niece or nephew. She smiled her famous smile and asked, "Why are you crying?" She seemed so happy. All I could do was sob because I knew she was not in the world anymore. I was so happy to see her and yet completely devastated.

That was many years ago. Reflecting on it now, it's still so vivid and clear but I think I finally get the message. Every day on earth is a blessing and another opportunity to live life fully, like Selena did. Instead of blaming my past shortcomings on hardships experienced in my youth, I can take all the moments that I've lived, happy and sad, good and bad, and acknowledge that each of them has made me who I am today. My faith in God, my husband and family, my friends and experiences, and my music have shaped me into a vibrant woman, an overcomer, a survivor, and I smile at her every time I look in the mirror. You go girl! We really only have today. It's time to sing again.

Another Message for the Reader

A few years ago, I had an incredible experience. I saw Father God in heaven! I know, I know, that is very hard to believe. I felt the same way as I was looking at Him! I can't explain why it happened other than I was seeking Him, and He decided to appear to me. I will forever be humbled by the experience, and it is my mission to tell everyone His message. Why? Because He told me to and He has been too good to me. I want you to experience all His goodness too.

My Vision of God on His Throne

It was a Sunday in late September, Lawrence and I had just finished packing up from a camping trip we took to celebrate his birthday. Before we left, I decided to go outside of the tree cottage where we were staying and have time with God. As I stood on the ground looking up into the sky, I could not believe what I saw or Who was staring back at me. What does it mean to gaze or look at God, I wondered? With an open heart, I decided to look up and search the sky for just that, a glimpse of God. As my eyes searched over the tree line, what happened next, I would never forget. I saw a pair of sandaled feet that were at the base of a flowing white robe. I saw two hands and arms resting on each armrest of a White Throne. Continuing to look up, I saw a white silky beard combed to a point. As I looked on, I saw more silky hair, wavy and blowing in the breeze. Then came the eyes; Eyes of jasper, glowing in bright light.

"My little one." He says gently with a smile.

Me, mouth gaping wide, no sound, not even a blink of the eyes. If I did blink, would I miss it?

"Little one, tell them. Tell them that I am with them when they struggle. I see and feel every tear. They are not alone. I desire them to be with Me always. I desire all my little ones to be with Me forever. Tell them, little one, that I love them; that I am here for them always and will never leave them. Tell them, little one that I AM real. I AM real. I AM Real!"

He is real. And just like He was there for me and brought me from under the dark cloud, He will do the same for you. You can trust Him. He is for you and never against you. Seek Him, if you don't believe me, but seek Him with all your heart and He will reveal Himself to you. He is real.

When you look for me, you will find me.
Yes, when you seek me with all your heart,
I will let you find me, says the Lord.
Jeremiah 29:13 NIV

About the Author

Maritza Mejias-Ditzenberger debuts her first book expressing her life experience in two things that have taken the world by storm: Anxiety and Depression. Maritza began suffering anxiety and depression from an early age and constantly questioned God, why? After writing down her thoughts in a self-reflecting and healing manner, *Beyond the Dark Cloud* surfaced and her question was finally answered. She believes it has become part of her ministry to help those suffering with Anxiety and Depression, cheerfully accepting the task at hand. She lives in Maryland with her husband Lance Ditzenberger and they are very much part of their church community as leaders of a small Bible study. She is also living out her dream of singing for the Lord as part of her church's worship group.

To contact Maritza, email: <u>BeyondtheDarkCloud@gmail.com</u>

Milton Keynes UK
Ingram Content Group UK Ltd.
UKHW011043080324
439029UK00001B/108